This book is dedicated to my parents, who taught me what a Casa is in the first place (both Home and House), and to Marianna, who lives with me in Techno Casa for real, turning it into an inestimably precious experience.

Techno Casa – an introduction to

Bricks as Bits. That is to say: the final victory of objects is revealed in the total disappearance of each object. Mobile phones have replaced design in mediating our relation to the surrounding space. All the tools that surrounded us were dematerialized. To stay alive – and to survive the digital – objects have become invisible, and are often processed in their own narratives. The total powerpointization of any discourse between (for instance) human beings is the meta-narrative that a laptop offers of itself. Actually humans – dowsers of wifi – allowed the wave to propagate from objects to furniture, so that even the very idea of decor was reorganized. The military wing of the digital revolution was the transformation of every room into an office, in short: the complete officialization of the indoor. Modular office furniture – now present in every homely homelimbo – became widespread and turned into common heritage the choice of diplomacy as the only way of life. But we should not consider decor and architecture as two separate entities, even when we are led to consider the mind and the body as two separate entities (and even when the only prison that we are capable of accepting is the one that we have drafted for ourselves). Architecture is also facing the digital – considering the skyscrapers, one might say that it surely does so with its head-on. All our architecture has become a large system of display with a variable content. This is particularly clear in Berlin, from where I'm writing – observing the Potsdamer-platzerization of Schöneberg – and the transformation of the Tempelhof Airport into a park area destined for bird-watching. The conversion of the former industrial spaces offers the set for these flashbacks: the old industry – that which produces material objects – moves into geographic areas with a cheaper manpower, and the spaces that remain – once conceived to produce – became spaces of presentation, exhibition and sale. Many museums are an integral part of this process, which starts with the assumption of the economic sphere of the creative storytelling (and not vice-versa) of an economic determination of art. As, you might say, the symbolic value of the product – and not its exchange value – is the main source of profit. And the fact that we call it virtual economy does not surely presuppose that

it is transparent. On the contrary: it is visibly trying to get rid of architecture with consolidated
methods, such as out-sourcing and zero-stock...
just in time for the colonization of every moment.
Architects are manipulators of symbols and architecture is an interface that desperately asks for
content: it wants to be semanticized by our love
for being humans. If we pay attention, there are
some vertical surfaces that we are willing to rec-
ognize as barriers or walls, provided they offer
power outlets for recharging the battery of our
portable interfaces. And in doing so, through em-
pathy, architecture survives. Survives thanks to
its inert materials, which are all but inert even if
we always call them inert. The predisposition of
certain materials to accommodate moulds, moss-
es and lichens is there to remind us that there is
life in the brick, and that for every season there is
a different kind of sweat.

Techno Casa – Attachment 1,12 Kb

I was trying to fall asleep, and perhaps I've made it. I sleep many miles away from my body. I always need time to get away from it: long separations, farewell speeches, greetings to the day that goes, applauses to that which arrives. I was trying to fall asleep, and all of a sudden I get the feeling that someone is pointing a light at my face, the eyelids are a very thin threshold, the mind pretends to be busy with something else. I rapidly rejoin my body to wake up with a start. I cannot understand what is going on, I briefly check around but there is no one home. There is probably a storm outside the window. I stand still and it happens again – someone points a light at my face, and this time it is clear as day: a slight presentiment finds its way, a shiver of absolute desolation, the idea of being alone and minuscule but in the form of feeling. I raise my head above the pillow and look for a helicopter among the clouds, a flying machine fished out of my fantasies, but reconditioned and augmented by fiction. And these thoughts are accompanied by the roar of thunder, the soundtrack of a personal apocalypse under the sheets. Through the sound I understand that it was nothing but lightning. Even if I still can't comprehend how a flash managed to get into my eyes without burning anything along its way, at this time of night I am satisfied with such explanation: I let myself be embraced by the sound revelation that replaces the scientific evidence, and I immediately drop off. Now that it is clear, the storm outside the window keeps me company. And while waking up, still dazed, I told M. what happened – but I had no clear evidence – only flashes of light assisted by words. Some days after, a sunny day: I was at the window to make sense of the void caused by the sudden change of season. While approaching the windows I think about what others tell me about their own windows, about these moments when the world is understandable because it is inserted into a wooden frame that isolates some fragments. Or in the frame of the monitor's display, the touch screen – but that's another story. Now I recall what A. – who lives near the Central Station in Milan – told me; from his window – if I remember right – he followed from above, step by step, a man who was building his informal architecture: a house in the street. And this takes me straight to Naples, to the seaside. I was waiting for C. to pick me up with his car, and I occupied his delay by observing a camping tent positioned on a sidewalk, surrounded by sleeping dogs. Meanwhile a well-dressed man arrives with a shopping bag and bends down to caress the dogs' heads one by one, lowering himself to the sidewalk in a rhythmic manner, according to the size of the animal he caresses. Then he shouts towards the tent, and he does so repeatedly until someone answers back from inside. They have a brief vocal exchange that reaches my ears deprived of consonants. Then the man leaves the bag and departs, I hear the unmistakable sound of the zip of the tent but I don't see what happens because C. has arrived – perhaps a while ago – and saw me standing there, and is now repeatedly blinding me with the headlights of his vehicle. The light intrudes between my eyes and the tent because it bounces off the window of a bank. And maybe not in that moment, but at this precise instant I found a solution. Once S. told me that the high-rise building that is close to the Milan Central Station causes problems to the lower and older buildings around it. As the skyscraper is covered with mirrored windows, during the sunny days the rays bounce against it and crash onto the surrounding architectures, corroding the wooden frames of windows and shutters. These rays – that arrive relatively scattered – are grouped by the skyscraper's mirrored windows and returned to very precise directions, towards humans who did not ask for them but who maybe get a tan. Here's how the lightning reached my eyes that night: vertical mirrors that defy the clouds and multiply the city also rise in front of my windows. The tourist signs that tell the story of the skyscrapers to travellers reveal: FROM A GRAND HOTEL TO AN OFFICE BLOCK. Skyscrapers with a shiny skin, like mine during sleep. A flash returned from a willing architecture – that reorganizes the turbulent motions of the sky in a distracted but technically perfect way – acts as an intermediary between me, my sleep, and the unexpected stars. And perhaps – if every skyscraper is a part-time beacon – then this is not the end of History, but it's the end of Geography.

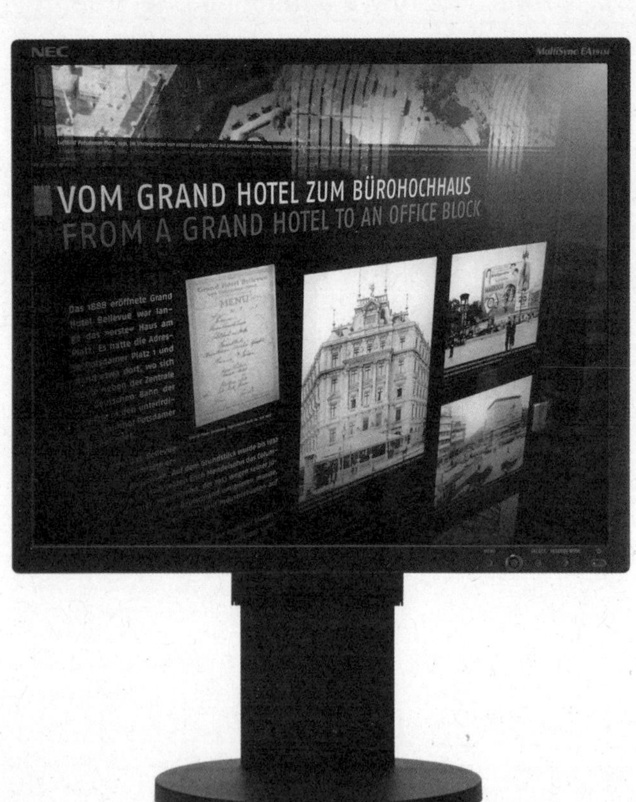
VOM GRAND HOTEL ZUM BÜROHOCHHAUS
FROM A GRAND HOTEL TO AN OFFICE BLOCK

Techno Casa – Attachment 2,29 Kb

I was on the phone with my mother – I was reading her horoscope, wanting to distract her from her life to distract myself from mine. Although I have a different zodiac sign – her horoscope seemed to be addressed to me. In effect I learned that the oldest known phrase is engraved on a jug of wine – in ancient Greek dating around 740 BC (the same Greece that is now strangled by the austerity policies of the European Union, exactly that same one)... The sentence reads: Which dancer is the most graceful one? – A different translation could be: Which dancer plays with highest grace? And which game are we talking about, if not that wonderful and horrible default operation that we have learned to call life? Rethinking it, it now seems clear that one of the best examples of a human being is that of a dancer – or simply – of those who know better how to synchronize with the game (to lead articulated partnerships with the ethereal). Nowadays the disappearance of the world of machines forces us to chase and presage renewed rhythmic solutions. Synchronization is not simply an adjustment – but the method by which a subject produces himself and – after his mother's act – he reinserts himself in the world. At stake is the inner autonomy of the body, and it is no longer about filling with this body those voids left vacant by the industrial process – or of adapting the body to inadequate postures, although the elbow holes on the desk attest to the opposite. It is rather about figuring out where – and when – are the machines, since they are supposedly invisible, perhaps they are no more – or perhaps they are everywhere, omnipresent: of dancing in silent times. As the dancer knows well, the search for a new rhythmic solution begins with the – self-inflicted – obligation of not believing in one's eyes, and of thus giving sense to emptiness, occupying it with the mind and body. The dilated echo of the whole history of Rave Parties hovers in this sentence. Or turning on the machines with the sound of new machines, reintroducing a noise in an architectural space that brings it back to life – while around it all is muffled. Inhabiting (dancing) ex-industrial spaces in ruins and reformulating the ritual – while stressing out the utter uselessness of the new temples. Because in those days gone the whole landscape was dotted by two kinds of ruins. Unfinished or abandoned buildings – but in both cases the same motivation: someone had forgotten the function of those half-architectures. They were architectural skeletons eroded by a fugue: the production of consumer goods was moving to areas where lower-cost labour ensured a greater profit, and here – in the meantime – came the society of service... and the machines? Became assets – invisible to the eyes. Where are they now, all those human bodies accelerated at full power – gathered in front of technology – in order to improve the flow of data? Where are the techno-dancers, now that their shared isolationism finally came true with the web? They are at the gym – listening to the music through their white-budded earphones. Are the white ear-buds the new white-collars? But – to make it clear – Rave Parties did not disappear due to the virtualization, volatilization of machines – they disappeared because of the extinction of the concept of the weekend. Thus, if one of the best examples of the human being is the dancer, who knows better how to synchronize with the game – it is because he is capable of recognizing the dispersion of that induced unity of time (choreography) known as the weekend. And this is not the feeling of a child, troubled by the fact that the world changes, but rather its opposite: this is a hypothesis of irreversibility – the perception of each detail of the spectrum of immobility... Who is synchronized to what and why, I can't see but I know it's there. It's a matter of time, of giving a before and an after to every event, to give it a meaning. No more ruins – but ourselves. Architecture became the place where it is easier to find a Wi-Fi connection, and the connection speed – or the amount of signal – is the unit of time. It is the typical countdown variable of every downloadable file – the streamlining of any communicative process between human beings, covered by the absolution of contingency. That said – let's dance, admitting no division between body and mind, let's dance and then sleep soundly.

Techno Casa – Attachment 3,19 Kb

The teacher was illustrating some ideas about the packaging of objects. He explained that there has been no relevant graphic innovation on the spines of books because they are displayed frontally – and not sidewise – in storefronts. Walking down the street, observing the bookstores' windows, I was amazed at the tendency to display repeatedly, side by side, many copies of the same publication – often a freshly printed novelty. The more it was a pocket book, the more it was necessary to multiply it to sell it, and thus the variable signboard of a shop that – apparently – sold a single product. This brings me back to that strange phenomenon of counterpoise – for which one ends up buying many books right when one does not have time to read them. In doing so – we offer ourselves a possibility in becoming, we honestly follow our vows – renewing votes of being better. The book – at the time of its purchase – is the spatiotemporal manifestation of our being in the world to which we tend by nature. When we will finally find the time to read it – we will be changed by then – but we will have physically built a part of ourselves that was rightly ours. In fact – as L. pointed out – we were led to consider buying a book as an ethically correct gesture even when (by necessity or virtue) the very idea of consumption (purchase of solutions) has been fully questioned. It ends up that books become part of the design of our rooms – their accumulation reminds us of a part of us ready to be awakened at any moment. Or they overlap verticalizing the time line – and increasing the volume of our fittings. Books, one might say, give a sense to furniture – they give ease to its modularity consisting of horizontal surfaces in constant expectation. And to think that this happens in a historical period in which publishing is challenged by the digital revolution – and reading on paper is becoming more and more an exquisite luxury. Perhaps the book is a gesture that defends architecture: its being in the world is a natural resemanticization of any room. If every book is a gesture that defends architecture – the reason why writing has become an extended practice in contemporary art it is now even clearer: we artists are committed to defend our workplace – and to prevent its eventual demise. The dissolution of architecture, in fact – its camouflage with the surrounding world of symbols – would strip the artist from the so-called appointed place, that which gives sense, one might say, to his product. As closing the factory to a workman – and turning that place into the shadow of a world that was, or rather, the projection of a human being in peace with the machines that he could have been. But the fact that nowadays artists write more means that they are more aware of their role within society, or – as F. pointed out – that their practices are becoming less effective – thus is their writing synonymous with frustration? Grammatical tears and the annihilation of life in speech. If there is the will we move ahead, if there is no will we write (or paint) – the ultimate (willy-nilly) goal is to meet with our fellows. It is not true that nowadays we write more because writing costs nothing – writing costs living – thus it costs nothing, not even technically. It is precisely in times of austerity that art should serve some purpose, and thus returns to chase its own functionality – even when the total loss of the real forces it to be an irrational functionality. For this reason language – writing – becomes part of the visual, as a default vehicle and information vector, as an attempt to meet as many people as possible. The trumpets sound: this is the great return of that technology in our society (very '90s) known as OCR – one that allows us to scan an image and read it as text... J. told me that every work is a gift that you donate to the world. Along the way I noticed that – as any gift you respect – it is wrapped in paper, and those who unwrap it to know what's inside are our peers. I imagined that a work of art could be a drawbridge to facilitate this encounter with our peers – and I only changed my mind recently: it is not a drawbridge but a trampoline, and if the encounter takes place, it takes place in total absence of architecture – it happens in mid-air.

Techno Casa – Attachment 4,82 Kb

I was walking in the monumental park – at night – it had been snowing for three days in a row. I noticed a strange alliance between the bronze sculptures and the evergreens. All in the dark and covered with snow. I could not understand who imitated what. If the sculptures resembled nature – or if the trees (flirting with my imagination) were not making fun of the sculptures, introducing them to the joy of living. Perhaps it is due to the ambivalence with which the snow covers the city. Everything is white – thus more calculable. But the distances, presences, plans disappear – and there is nothing left to be calculated – but time. In the iridescence of a surface that does not remain true to itself not even for a moment – the ease with which reference points are connected is increased by the complete disappearance of any reference point. Leaving the park, to my right I find the glass palace of the CDU – the union of the German Christian Democrats, epitomized by the current Chancellor Angela Merkel. And it is precisely in the glass of this building that I see reflected the facing architecture, the Bauhaus Museum. And at this point I ask myself: is the proximity of these two architectures – that face each other – really fortuitous, or do they belong to the same plan? And maybe this plan is way wider than the city planning? One thing is clear: the representative palace of the strength of the parliamentary majority – and the correspondent representative palace of the artistic movement that made of utilitarianism its standard – have arranged to meet here, at this traffic light, at this crossroads. What should they tell each other – or rather – what should they tell me, who got it now? If it is true that the cellphone has replaced furniture in the intermediation between ourselves and the surrounding space, it is equally true that politics (not the web) became the only true global technological interface. I conclude that the palace of the CDU and the Bauhaus Museum – the odd couple (joint venture) – are a coalition for a shared interest: to ensure that its people (target) continues to believe in interactive technology – and consequently in parliamentary representation. These days revolutions, as democracies, seem to want to change the world's perception of them as events – and instead do not seem to want to improve the living conditions of the human beings who live them. For this reason technological interactivity, seen from here, is a myth. It proposes to circumscribe the solutions by numbers – leading to the belief that some problems may be eliminated by doing so, in practice – this is nothing but the revival of the eldest method of total cancellation of minorities – that method which dehydrates life from the rivers of fear and from the vortexes of the incalculable. In a work context – this method results in the infinitesimal fragmentation of professions and professionalisms. This way each category or field of knowledge can refer to other categories or fields of knowledge for the research of a satisfactory result every time a doubt or hypothesis is likely to question its internal logic. In practice, we are constantly deferring – and in doing so – we end up in the depths of a constant and pathological desire to forecast. To wonder what will happen is the easiest method, in practice, to forget what is happening. But this involves everyone and never goes out of fashion, and can be found in every person who – so is said – has priorities. Clouds of sense play at being solid geometries – and then are sold as scales of values ... but what does a scale of values really mean? It means the time in which a person (depending on agility and contingencies) is capable of climbing up or down this scale in more or less speed. We can only build a scale of values by admitting that some steps will always be missing – and that this causes holes and voids that are never where we remember them – moreover, this scale has no handrails. In the iridescence of a surface that does not remain true to itself not even for a moment – the ease with which reference points are connected is increased by the complete disappearance of any reference point. At the moment we are all unable – unlike the snow – of taking care of everything.

Techno Casa – Attachment 5,53 Kb

The day I was born my father was somewhat afraid that I would arrive with protruding ears like his – as a lad his friends called him Dumbo. When my grandfather arrived to the hospital – my father welcomed him with a smile – he was happy, certainly happy for the contained dimension of my auricular pavilions. The father of my father placed a hand on his shoulder (I picture him mocking) and told his son not to worry: those small ears, my small ears, would bloom like two roses in the sun. And to this day, rather than standing there watching the trees that obstinately stay in line against the tempest, or the seagulls that get close to the shore without flapping their wings, I rather have my ears shaping the wind. If, as they say it, the ideas are in the air, it is the merit of the wind – but first because of the ears, and then of the mouth. When we sleep one ear is always leaning on the cushion, making it impossible to hear sounds in stereo. Maybe we meet and mate to avoid this unidirectional trap, to choose a sleeping partner that offers another pair of ears and that allows us to hear normally, even as we sleep (and we could even say that the same unidirectional – single channel – trap is produced by the substitution of the human gaze with that of webcams). Perhaps the tree branches do not wriggle because of the sun – attempting to expose themselves to its rays – not even because of the wind. The branches of the trees grow following the movement of the clouds: those that point downwards were probably born in the winter, trying to follow the manifestations of the true – terrain – by moving away from the fog. Each branch remembers its own cloud, and day after day it follows and listens to it, attempting to point it out to the other branches, which in their turn are intent on their own clouds. We cannot speak about an out-and-out escape attempt from the trunk, but surely without the stubbornness of the branches we would remain unaware of the constant peregrination of clouds. The wind that moves the clouds and the leaves in the trees produces a very similar sound to that of the sea waves that bring the debris during the low tide – and both movements, from many points of view, measure time. But wind is unpredictable – and leads us toward an incalculable repetition to which we cannot get used. And by the way: were we brought up to repeat gestures – or did someone try to transmit to us ideas that underlie them, in order to give life to unprecedented gestures? Each one forgives something to their predecessors and each one gives something to their successors. We forgave them for having believed in the fable of the multiplication of bread and fish – because we understood that it is a refined stratagem based on the fact that breadcrumbs are infinitely divisible. And we also forgave them for believing that it would be simple to get everyone to agree – because it became clear that we can only get to a common agreement when someone is absent. Now all we can do is to shape the wind, eavesdropping on the daily chatter that each leaf has with its own branch. Each one forgives something of their predecessors and each one gives something to their successors. And to save something, perhaps, on the passing from the arms to the mind – from the farmhand to the independent cognitive labourer. From the time of the seasons to the time of machines, and then to the time of the mind: listening to the wind as a provisional formula – invisible barricades against the colonization of the moment. From the time of the seasons to the time of the machines, and then to the time of the mind: after wedding mechanics, agriculture remarried chemistry – apparently a less demanding girl. Agriculture in the role of the husband – that husband who, in order to have his cake and eat it, tucked his wife into the cake, only to realize that by doing so he could not make love to her. Love as the intimate challenge to fleeting time – and at the same time – solidification of its own labyrinth, through a reciprocal externalization of subcutaneous sensations.

Techno Casa – Attachment 6,69 Mb

I'm observing a drop of olive oil which, setting out from my wrist, moves along my forearm to the elbow where it dreams of turning into a stalactite, in spite of the fact that it is visibly losing volume and consistency along the route it is tracing on the pores of my skin. Following the drop as it diminishes I tell myself that I, daily, am working for the Rubbish Collection Service. Each time I deal with the differentiated collection of my garbage I am working for the Rubbish Collection Service and they don't pay me. It particularly annoys me to spend time on this, just as it does to have to put my hands into a plastic bag which emanates the stench of various foodstuff containers. I have been advised – precisely by the Rubbish Collection Service – to wash these containers, these tins of exhausted air which look to me like damp coffins awaiting the return of their corpses. So I have to clean up the differentiated waste before putting it in the bag that I keep in the cupboard under the sink, and since the packaging has been done for my eyes, it seems that there is no doubt: it's my own duty to wash it. In practice I clean, divide, pack up and then subdivide and put it in the special bin, because taking responsibility for the waste you produce is a necessary step towards the planet's survival. Even the wealthiest multinationals in the food sector think this way, often anticipating in point of fact the application of a future legislative theory on the subject. A company that makes a famous fizzy drink – for example – in a South American country has set up a pilot project to have its bottles recovered directly by Waste Pickers – a particularly straitened class of self-employed workers – whose main task is exactly the one I complained about above. Each of the Waste Pickers has a zone, often a street. In the morning they arrive outside the houses to collect the family garbage and maybe, who knows, they are thanked for it but they are certainly not paid (exactly like my situation with the Rubbish Collection Service). Then the Waste Pickers spend the day sorting the contents of the bags, anticipating the gesture with which, the same evening, they will divide and pile up the coins according to size, the cents earned by selling plastic, metal, glass and paper to recycling companies. F. tells me that it is impossible to imagine

– due to current hygiene regulations – that the company which makes the famous fizzy drink is buying back its bottles to be washed and reused. And, F. reaffirms, it is equally unthinkable that the company recovers them in order to transform them into raw material for the production of new bottles, because there are other firms specialized in this sector that can offer the service at a decidedly lower price. So, I say to F., we might imagine that the real motivation is an attempt to digitalize reality through rubbish. In fact the company that produces the famous fizzy drink – gathering its bottles through the Waste Pickers – obtains spatial-temporal information about consumption of its product because it can trace (with an approximation very close to the facts) where the drink has been consumed and in how much time – when was the last drop of the famous no longer fizzy drink definitively drunk? Having obtained these data and correlated them with production and distribution data the company can forecast the desire for the fizzy drink – also obtaining a magical lucrative power due to voracious farsightedness which in turn is backed up by a mathematically intransigent calculation presented in the form of environmentalist sentiment. And each time I surf the web I allow anyone at all to forecast some wish of mine. Each movement of my finger – known as a click – produces information for someone else and therefore future earnings:

this is how the rules of the web are transferred to the reality – to all effects phenomenal – of rubbish. This process allows consumers (users) to give meaning to their free time by transforming it into unpaid work, and to separate – once and for all – the idea of productivity from that of employment. So it is no longer true that you pay for everything, since especially on the web there are increasingly more free services, but they are there because we have unconsciously accepted the idea of obligatory and extensive voluntary work. Among other things, giving meaning to your free time by transforming it into unpaid work is an activity which until recently was exclusively for the aristocracy – which is why we are all trying it today – click – and all succeeding – double click. This is the pulpit from which the sermon of the entire middle class comes with regard to its own subsistence. We might then replace the question: from which pulpit does the sermon come? — With the question: from which sermon does the pulpit come? I pause for a moment and actually regret having complained about my lack of free time, but just as I am mentally reconciling myself with the Rubbish Collection Service an unconditioned movement of the neck escapes all control – and I find myself licking my forearm, catching that lost drop of olive oil.

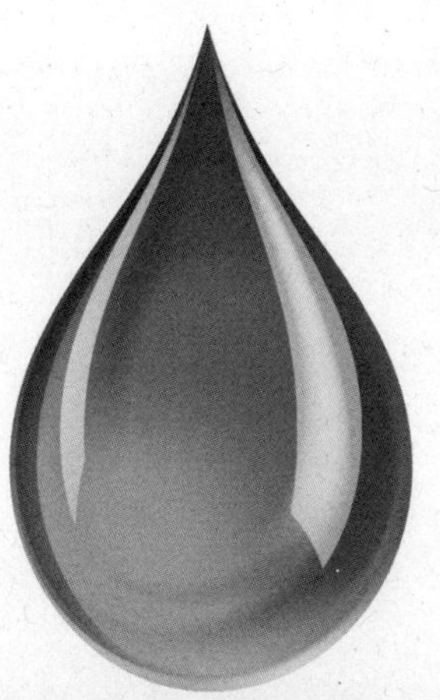

– Each notable change in fashionable music is the index of a change in the most important provisions of the State.
– How does this strange relationship come about? […]
– By "simple taking root". One sings to oneself, listens, repeats. The new rhythm spreads through everyday life where it is strengthened.

Alain Badiou, Plato's Republic

Here you can also purchase songs which the shopkeeper sings and the customer must retain in his head; but this is usually easy since they are very old songs which have become boring by being sung so much. They are bought mainly by young people in love […] the songs are accessible to everyone, and usually after purchasing one the young man goes out singing it at the top of his voice. The shopkeeper rushes to the door to correct the out of tune parts, but the young man doesn't listen and goes back over the song in his own way as he roams around town singing. Everybody knows what that singing preludes.

Gianni Celati, Fata Morgana

Techno Casa – Attachment 7,02 Mb

The more I listen to the latest Daft Punk album the more I realize that it represents a new idea of the present: as if it were a sound documentary on what has happened – but created with the ears of becoming. It codifies the musical event in a precedent – thus letting the listener savour the idea of being himself its duration – the during. As if they were no longer selling discs, selling music – but selling the dream of becoming musicians. As if the digital revolution had covered the planet with an ethereal surface of impartiality – allowing anyone to create music and make it heard everywhere by means of the web. At a concert for example only the musicians take part – and if we want to divide them into two groups there would be active musicians – on stage – and passive musicians – beneath the stage. The Daft Punk album is an educational disc – a fuse – every fuse is a chain – a fuse connected to sound explosives which at the moment however are only in the study phase. The laboratories where these sound explosives are in the study phase are called, precisely, rooms – and in them are new generations of musicians who are right now moving their heads to the rhythm of their latest creation. They shake the whole house with vibrations – as if destroying it rather than getting out of it were enough to go travelling! This however – it must be said – is a hallucination created by the ghost that lurks within every musical instrument, in every technological interface used for making music. In fact these instruments – while on the one hand they perfectly furnish the room (finding the ideal place in every chosen place) – on the other hand were created to facilitate transportation requirements, often to the extent of being pocket-sized. Not by accident, whether I'm at home or away I listen to the Daft Punk album only on my smartphone – just like the latest from Jay-Z, one of my favourite rappers. But it's a different story here because Jay-Z did this album through an app produced exclusively for the company that made and marketed my smartphone. With this app I downloaded the album free, a full three days before the record company's official launch, and Jay-Z sees this method as a genuine possibility for reformulating the wild rules of the web. It's well known that the internet produce leaks – and that often the most eagerly expected albums appear in free illegal download even before they are completed. We might say that Jay-Z did nothing else than sell the album leak to a multinational phone company which in turn guaranteed the rapper advanced sales of a million copies to give its customers, myself included. So Jay-Z ensured that his new release would go platinum even before it came out, creating a precedent in record industry history. In a word, the rapper branded a leak. And the sponsoring of a leak – evolution in an auto-poietic key of the trite agree to the sale of the scoop – must have been food for thought for a dear friend of Jay-Z's who is also president of the United States. If Barack Oh Blah Blah had followed his friend's example – branding the numerous leaks his government has had to face – he would probably have managed to gain a great economic benefit, I tell myself. In the climate of a permanent statistical survey the idea is to make everything mimetic and transparent – vaporized: clouds the same colour as the sky pass by – and how can you see them? As if they didn't buy votes any more – but sold the dream of becoming a member of parliament. The avant-garde attitude in western democracies – the transmutation of a new technology in the very lively form of a political party – is no other than affirmation of the fact that any type of abstraction can be experienced as the original parliamentary abstraction. In this way I find out that Jay-Z has a gig in town so I decide to follow the melody – just as you do when you hear a phone ringing that isn't your own but you'd like to answer it anyway. I find myself in a part of the city built recently and swiftly turned into a piazza with view to drawing the eyes of we bipeds towards the glass facade of the arena that hosts great events. This building seems to have just arrived – and the dust it raised on landing transformed at once into cement – immobilized in a vertical parcelling out of the spaces – blocked in the form of a clearance sale. As if they no longer rented out flats but sold the dream of becoming owners. As if the alliance between the property sector and finance – faced with a punishing welfare state – had fluidified the mechanism of social compensation through private debt, seen as the ultimate method of access to shared property. And what is the address of these new flats up for sale? When I found it, looking for a solution in the form of a street sign, I didn't want to believe my eyes: not only the name of the arena but also the name of the piazza itself where the architecture stands is precisely the name of my phone company, the one where I pay my phone bills! Then – flabbergasted – I go into the arena and realize that it is all set around the transparent facade whose glass – riveted with the stratagem of grid repetition – is supposed to refer to the possibility that the world herein is a fair representation of the world out there. I'm surrounded by new wretched building materials – rendered organic by a whirl of LEDs as if to manifest a perfect marriage between energy saving and semiotic waste – as if for example the White House got its name for being built completely in plasterboard. Then fortunately everything disappears: the lights go out and thousands of mobiles are switched on – Jay-Z comes on stage and I let myself be embraced by the general roar – each concert is the meta-narration which the participating smartphones offer of themselves.

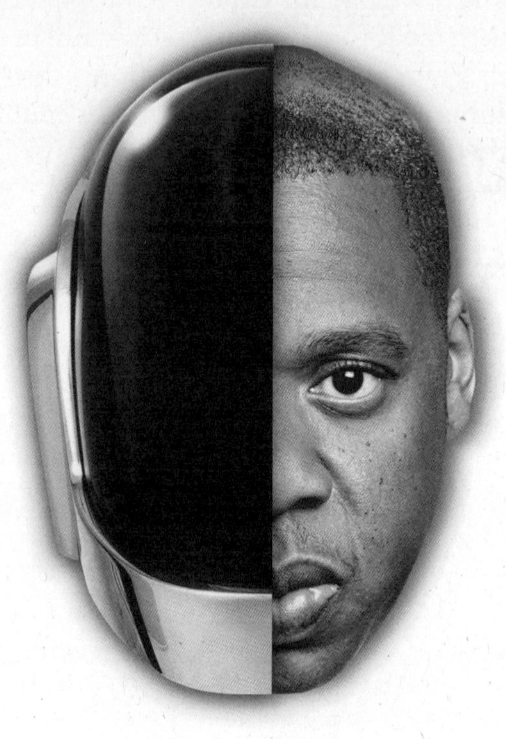

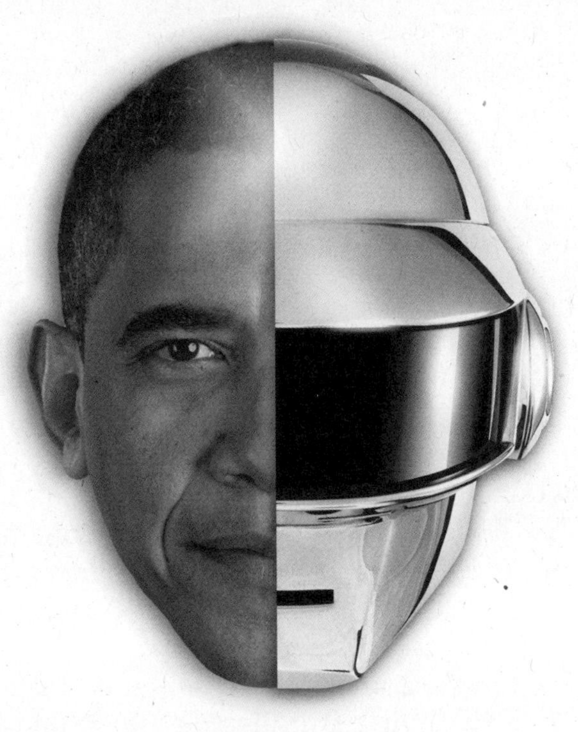

Techno Casa – Attachment 8,88 Mb

I check the news on my smartphone every three minutes. I read only the headlines, without going into depth. I assure myself that the world out there is unchanged – or I make sure that if anything should happen out there then at least it has little to do with me. I rarely allow myself a printed newspaper, but when I happen to do so I treat it like luxury goods and inspect the slightest details. Among the various ads competing in the corners of the daily that I am now paging through – there is one that really grabs me. A company specialized in transforming any bathtub into a shower unit. I think for a moment and say to myself that I have never considered this possibility – transforming the bathtub into a shower. In effect – apart from people with motory problems or owners of Jacuzzis – who still takes a bath? I think of K. – K. is one of the few people I know who still possesses a bathtub. One day she revealed to me that in winter – after a successful day's work, she awards herself a special prize by taking a long hot bath, after having switched off her smartphone. I remember that when K. put her new smartphone into my hands she checked – blushing slightly – to see if they were clean. Then she said to ignore the mess – pay no attention to the stupid apps scattered here and there: she'd downloaded them for her son who plays with them now and then. I remember that when K. invited me to dinner with the excuse of showing me her new home – as soon as I crossed the threshold she asked me – blushing slightly – to remove my shoes. Then she said to ignore the mess – pretending here and there to chase the cause of it who – in the unanimous opinion of the adults present – was her son – now hiding behind the washing machine in the kitchen. K. told me she had no choice – when she moved in the flat already had both tub and shower – so she kept the tub, and instead of not using it at all she at least used it from time to time. The tub occupied more than two square metres – making the bathroom smaller and less practicable – hence the washing machine in the kitchen. Now that I take a closer look at the advertisement for the firm that transforms bathtubs into showers – I note that in the logo there's a man laying a sort of shiny hatch on the bathtub. This man is a well trained technician – you understand this from the fact that he's wearing red dungarees with the braces crossed at the back – an image which immediately refers to the coherence of physical and manual work. With my smartphone I do an internet search and – while waiting for the webpage to appear – I note that the circular icon turning on itself centre screen looks like the door of a functioning washing machine. The firm's website finally opens and I discover that the time necessary for the man in the red dungarees to transform a bathtub into a shower is exactly 8 hours. I imagine that after 8 hours of work that man is left with another 8 for leisure and 8 for sleep... but just as I'm thinking it I already feel I'm wrong. This punctuation of the 24 hours in three blocks of 8 hours belongs – I tell myself – to a period of history when flats didn't have showers, only bathtubs. What happened in practice is that the bathtub rose to its feet – becoming a shower – precisely when the number 8, tired of itself and its repetition, lay down on its side – becoming more or less like this ∞ – the symbol of infinity. In fact the number 8 was never able to rest – it's only now that the bathtub has stood up that the number has the space to stretch out – like this ∞. And I would not be amazed tomorrow to discover that other friends – to avoid installing the washing machine in the kitchen and leave the number 8 to rest in ∞ – had decided to do without both bathtub and shower – because you can always clean up in the gym, at the swimming pool, at your workplace. The idea of furnishing (a flat with furniture) could be replaced by the idea of customisation (of the smartphone with apps) – as if emptying your home of now useless objects instead of accumulating them were the formula for never ageing.

Techno Casa – Attachment 9,24 Mb

Yesterday I bought a brand of cigarettes I'd never tried, because the ones I usually smoke were out of stock. Opening the packet I was amazed to find a message inside. On a small card with a blue background, which immediately recalls the European flag, there was a statement followed by a question: Smokers discriminated against! What else? Then turning it over I realized that it was an actual complaint against the regulations the European Union is formulating on the dispensing of tobacco, a complaint that sets out on a peremptory explanation that made me smile and foresee the establishment of a smokers' trade union subsidized by the tobacco companies. The words on the card are: we feel that the European Union should occupy itself with more important things! This is such a generic statement that everyone can only agree, and identifying them as a group of consumers only reminds Europeans what Europe is for. Such a generic idea of Europe that everyone can only agree. I wonder what they really have in common, these Nations that have united, and I ask myself if, when one stands together, one does so to achieve the best or to share the worst. For example if I say: with difficulty simple! – And then I say: simply difficult! – Why does evil always win? Now my thoughts go back to R. – who told me that she smokes a lot of cigarettes – greatly enjoying them – but only in dreams. Has R. maybe found the solution to every evil? If I had to make an effort to find what these European Nations have in common I could not help thinking of the architecture of their suburban areas – and of its being a volumetric reflection of a process of abstraction that has brought us to this point only to let us off even if it is not the terminus. A process of abstraction that has led to investment no longer in tangible property (a house) – but in immaterial goods (stocks and shares) – a process which then folded in on itself precisely because immovable property – so evidently immovable in suburban areas – has remained over time the fertile soil on which hopes are cultivated. In fact love, after being condensed in the act of creating a new family, is crystallized in the architecture represented by the new home. Families began working in factories – from the countryside they moved to the city – bearers of life to threshold zones, now urbanized with diligence – crookedly cut out with the town-planning scissors – and then dismally pasted around arterial roads (symbol of civilization). These commuter areas are called 'dormitory quarters' in Italian because those who live there spend their lives dreaming. In these quarters the nearer you are to a heavy traffic intersection the greater the cost of your home, quite apart from its specific features. The anthropological deformation of a species begins with awareness of the fact that a balcony overlooking an underground station or bus stop is preferable to a balcony overlooking the open countryside – also because, it is said, new buildings will soon rise on those uncultivated fields. So the balcony overlooking the underground station not only offers a secure and stable townscape but also certifies – like a wedding or a funeral – the fulfilment of a destiny. But over and above public transport – which is not enough to meet new needs and certainly does not glorify the fulfilment of a destiny – the asphalt has arrived there like a pedestal on which to exhibit cars: their chromatic glimmering perfectly multiplies the blinding reflections of the dream that roams around the car parks quiet as you like: mute areas with lonely lampposts that look about themselves as if something could change, lampposts that flirt with trees without realizing that it will never work. The cars change the dimensional scale: their leather interiors extend outside the rooms – towards society – leather sofas: as if several people could sit on the same sofa without being squeezed. And so the car parks are repeated one after the other – and often surround the bases of the buildings, bearing out that social construction is well fixed in the ground. And meanwhile – there in the factories – the machines function so well that they function too much (overproduction). Machines for the workers – like (non-European) carers for wives – arrive as help but then become replacements. And it will be the machines themselves that interpret a new type of chlorophyllian process – like the streetlamps that flirt with the trees in car parks... Did you really think that trees reddened only in autumn? Just as vegetation was necessary to man (feeding on carbon dioxide – which human beings expel – but expelling oxygen – which human beings need to live) so machines are necessary to man because they feed on quality time – which human beings expel – and expel numerical time – which human beings need to live better, to do more things and continue desperately to rail against passing time as if indecipherable fortunes had been lost. And I could go on forever and a day – but I smoke the last one and move on my way.

Techno Casa – Attachment 10,01 Mb

I watch the development of the summer storm from the window. I focus on a building and exclude from my vision everything around it which – every day – suffers and enjoys its shadow in rotation. Although behind the building the clouds pursue one another, blend into new anthropomorphic configurations and then suddenly part forever, I have a clear sensation that they are stationary – and that it's the building that moves. Just as on a train stopped at the station I perceive a false movement due to that fact that – outside the window – a carriage on the next platform has set off, in the same way the building is the protagonist in perennial movement onstage, whereas the sky is immobile, the most ancient of stage backdrops. As soon as the storm calms down – to get back a moment of life in this desk death – I decide to go running in the park. I get wet in a rain I am already forgetting and find the park mournful, a puddle of water in total absence of the din of kids, enveloped in the shadow of other new building sites. All at once it is clear to me what impels the lost solitary walkers, apparently old people with nothing to do, to observe these building sites with such interest: at those moments, dictated by the rhythm of building mechanics, the architecture is alive – where setting up the site is mise-en-scène – movement. Moving cranes are metal carriers that geographically localize the novelty and their central gantry (x-axis) fixes the roots while the jib, which is detached from the body (y-axis), prematurely announces the boundaries. While running I realize that ahead of me in the distance some rays of sunlight have made their way to sunset and illuminate solely a bench that seems the size of a kingdom and temporarily in-habited by a queen who – enclosed in an invis-ible but iridescent cocoon – is reading a highly important book. Glimpsing her from afar – in the perspective allowed by my running – I not only seemed to know her but I also had the sensation – wholly false – that she was reading the book of my life. When my running body entered into that ray of light I turned my back on the queen – who in the meantime might also have dissolved – and my face veered sharply towards the sun – my eyes met the source of the rays and tried desperately to focus on the trembling spherical form. I could say that what I experienced, in feeling the mucus in my nose dry up in an instant and distil drops of pleasure down into my throat – was a sensation altogether like an orgasm – amplified by my sweating and being totally strained from the run. Thenceforth the course of the run was dictated by the search for that sensation – which I was able to feel again, not diluted but intensified by the absence of surprise reaffirmed in repetition. The passage of time, just like travelling in space – I told myself – obliges you to put yourself at ease. Sometimes the first thing you do is to rediscover sensations you already know, but in new times – or to relocate things ascertained in places never before crossed. You see the features of your best friend in a passer-by, or you breathe the air of spring even if it is late summer – you somehow seek to make yourself at home. And you hang onto everything, but really everything: the more reality becomes unliveable the more you invent something that doesn't exist, or rather you make an effort to glimpse something that hasn't yet happened but at the same time is a mixture of things taken for granted. This, we might say, is the formula with which – at the apex of a need – something new comes about. Something that hasn't yet happened but at the same time is a mixture of things taken for granted. And actually this is the carrier with which we human beings head in the direction of a better life. And precisely for these reasons love cannot but be a slow sliding backwards – or a race in constant syncopation that brings us back to our point of departure. Where did we set out from? We set out by going to sleep with our feet entangled but back to back. Whereas the next night we fell asleep barely grazing each other's lips so as not to lose even a moment. The longest day of the year without calling it solstice. Then in the morning the only thing there to show us that time had not wholly stopped was the slightly grown beard and not knowing how to respond to that new tickling of the inner thigh. Years later – walking the street by night – we once more talked of that moment, observing it in a precise object that emerged from a historic building. An old sundial had been installed at the back of the Museum. A special streetlamp – set on the building opposite – illuminated it with a circle. So the sundial gave always and only one time of day forever – all night because it was illuminated by a fixed object – the streetlamp – instead of the tireless sun. And this streetlamp which threw light on it actually underscored its artificial being – short-circuiting its function. Then again the storm, and we were drenched by a rain we were already forgetting.

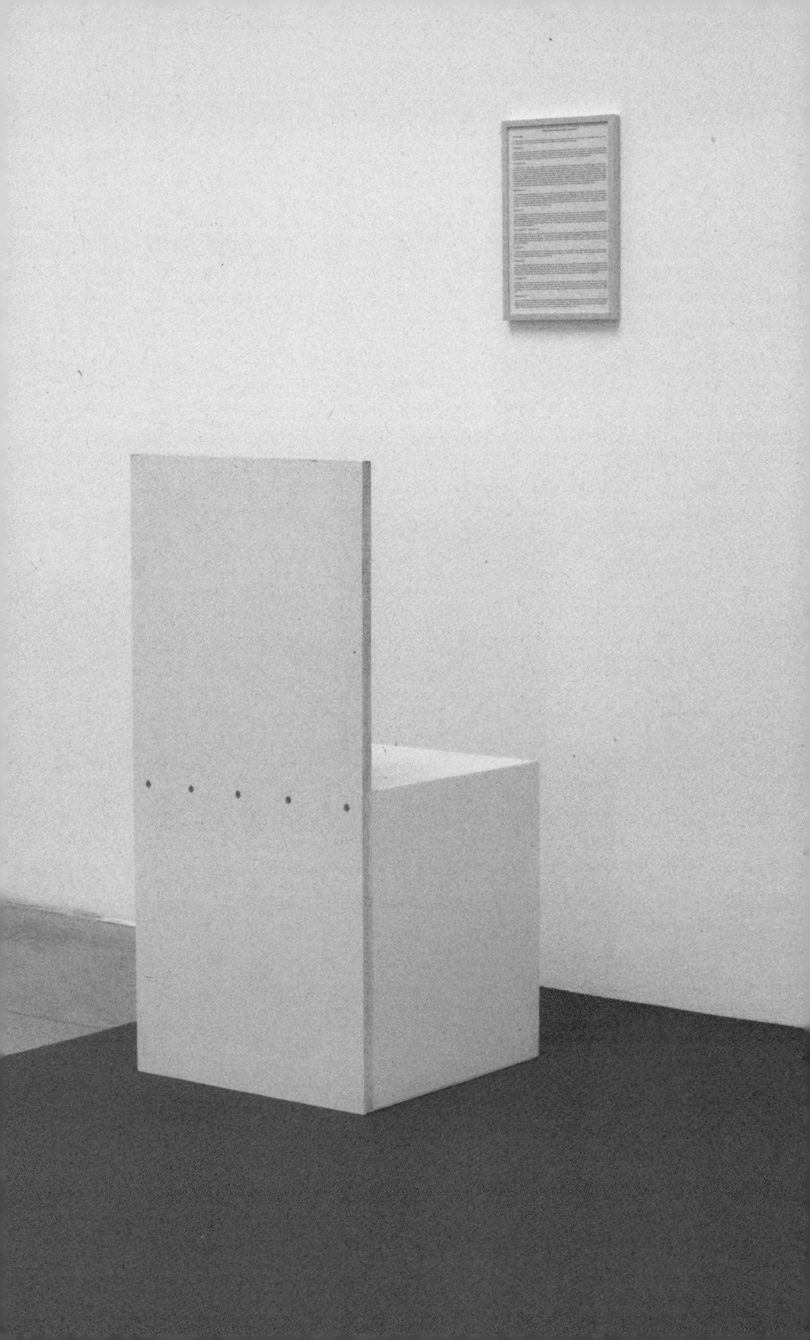

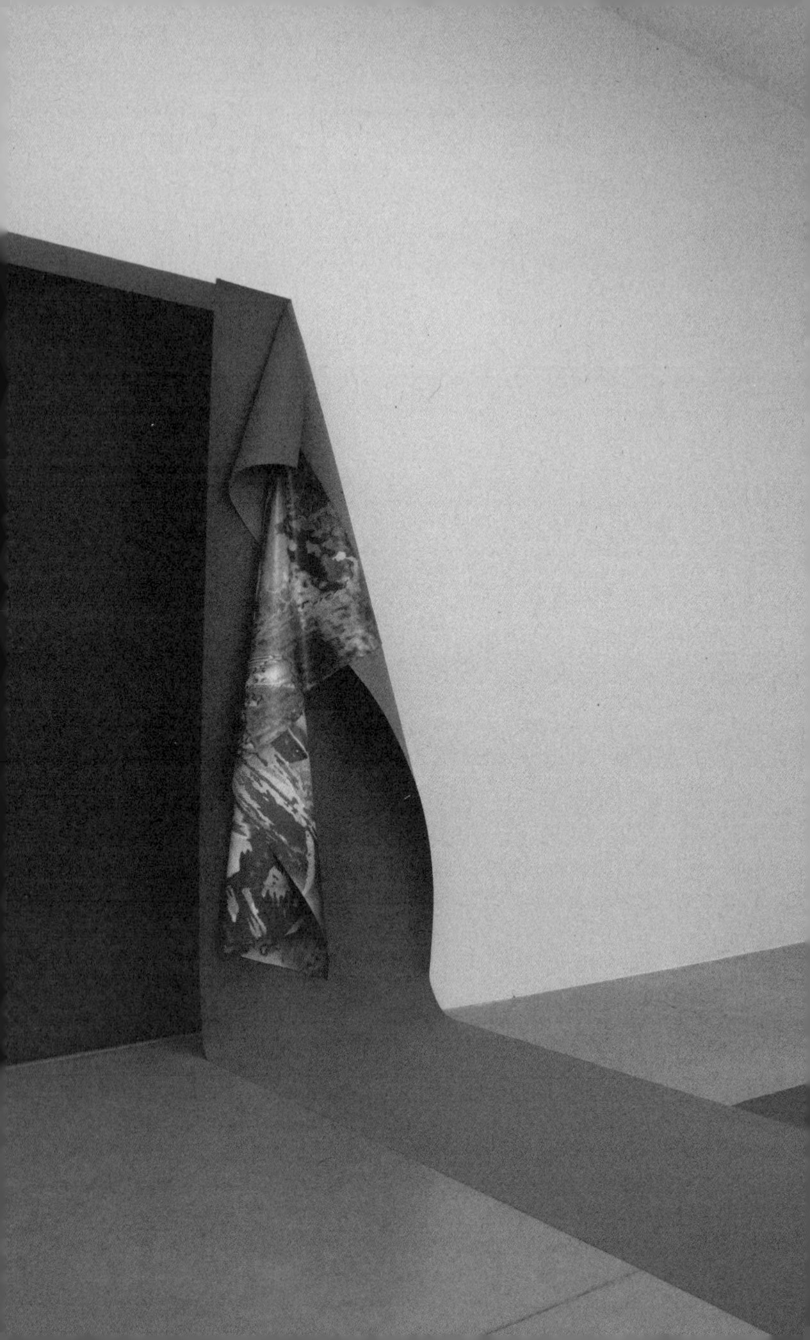

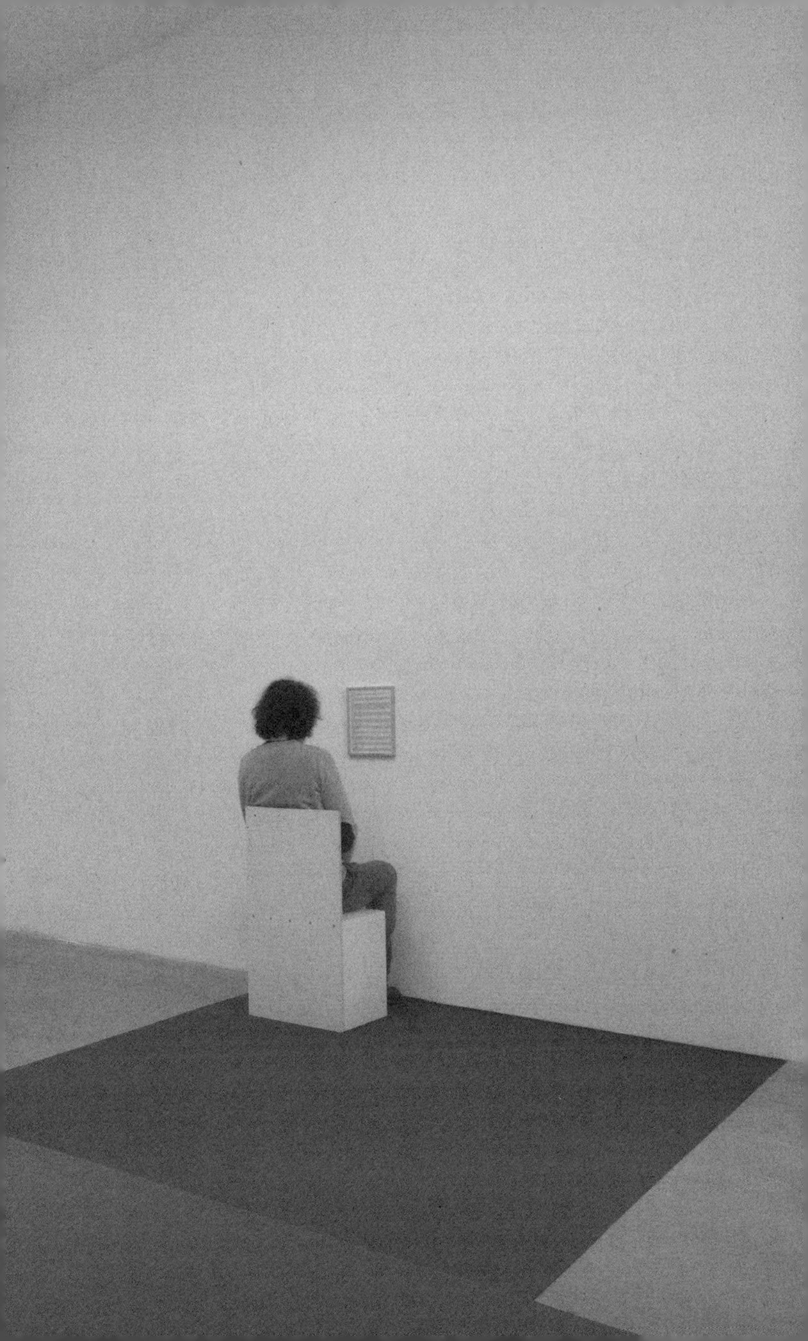

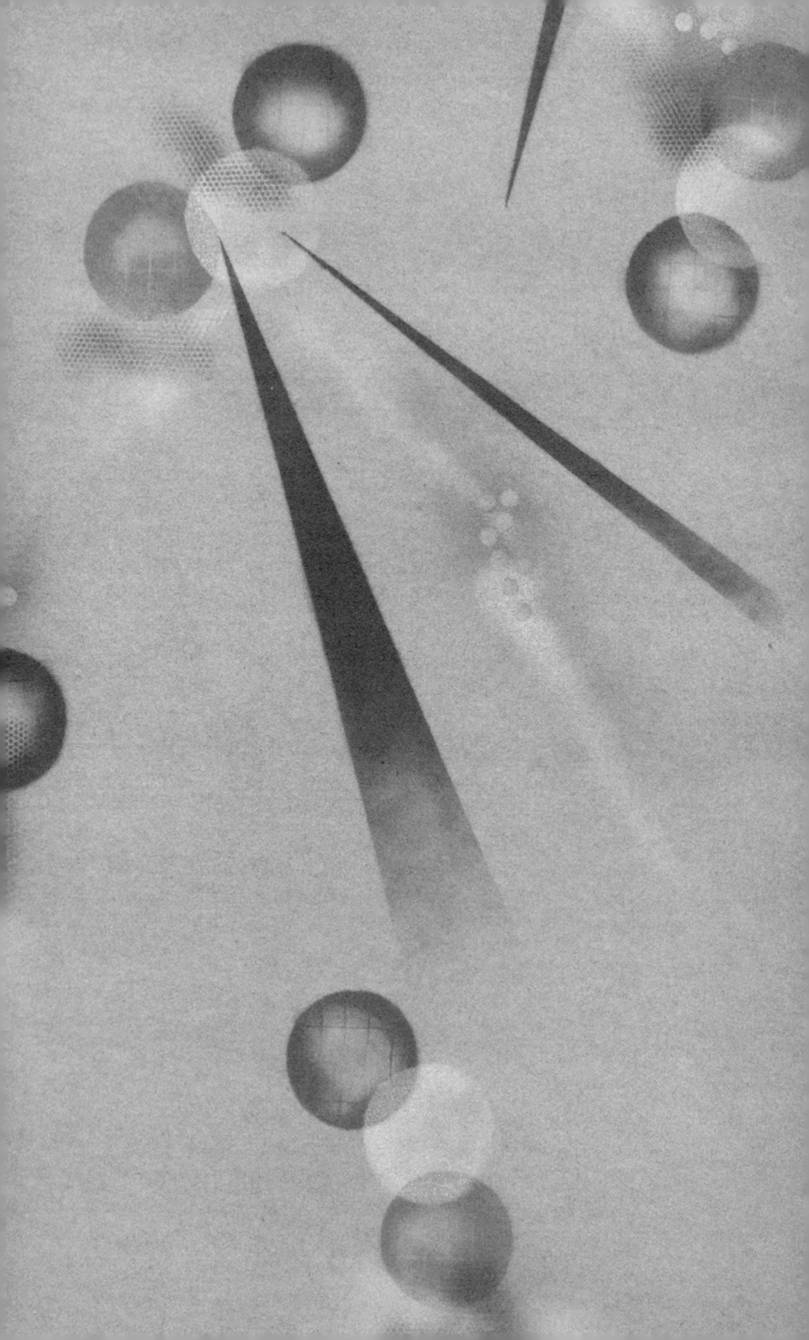

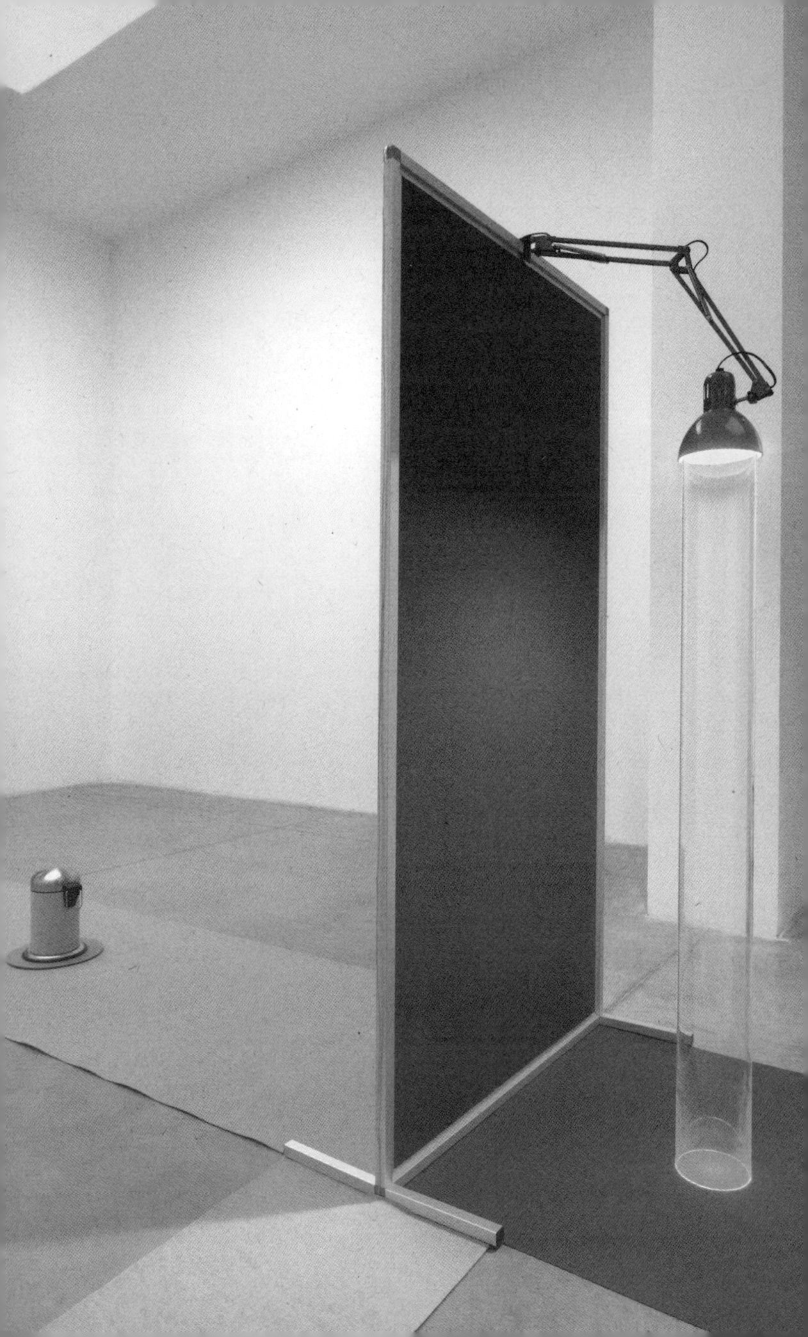

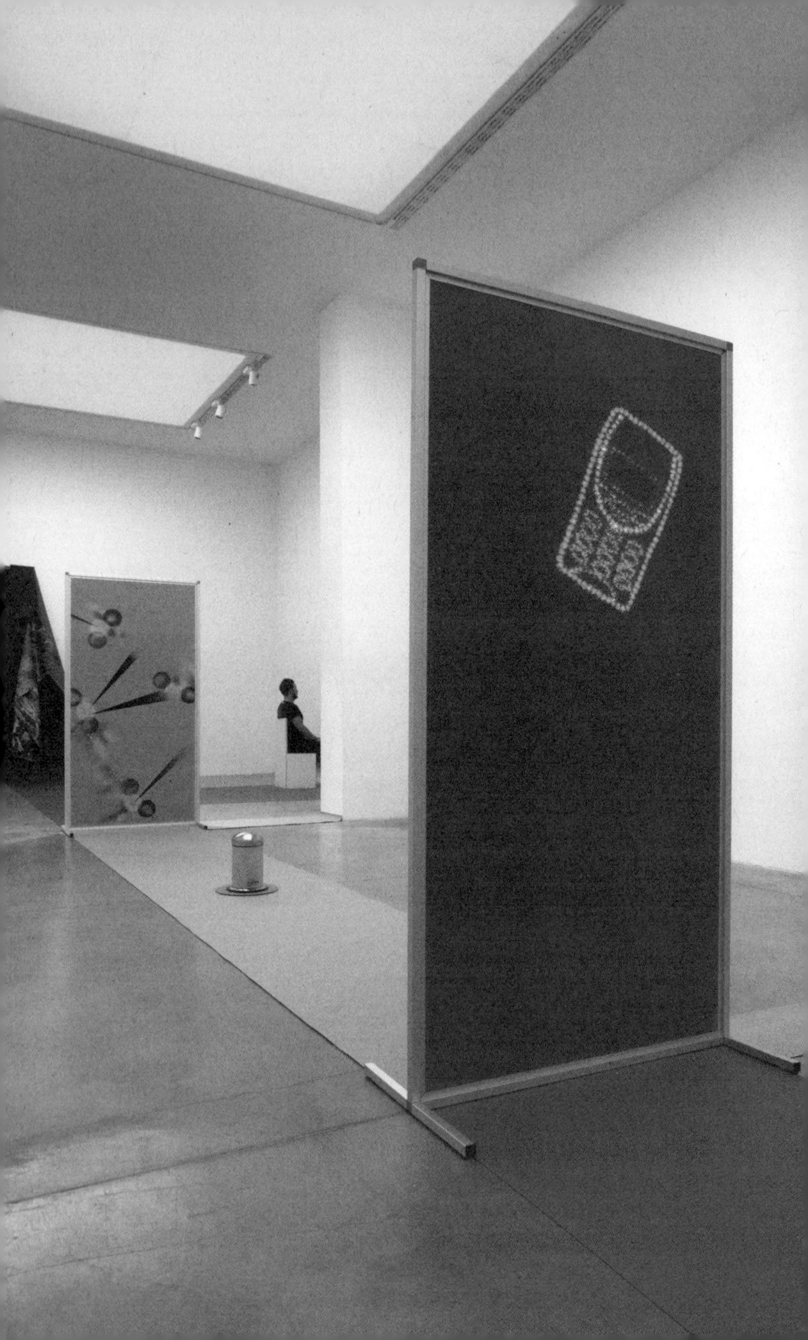

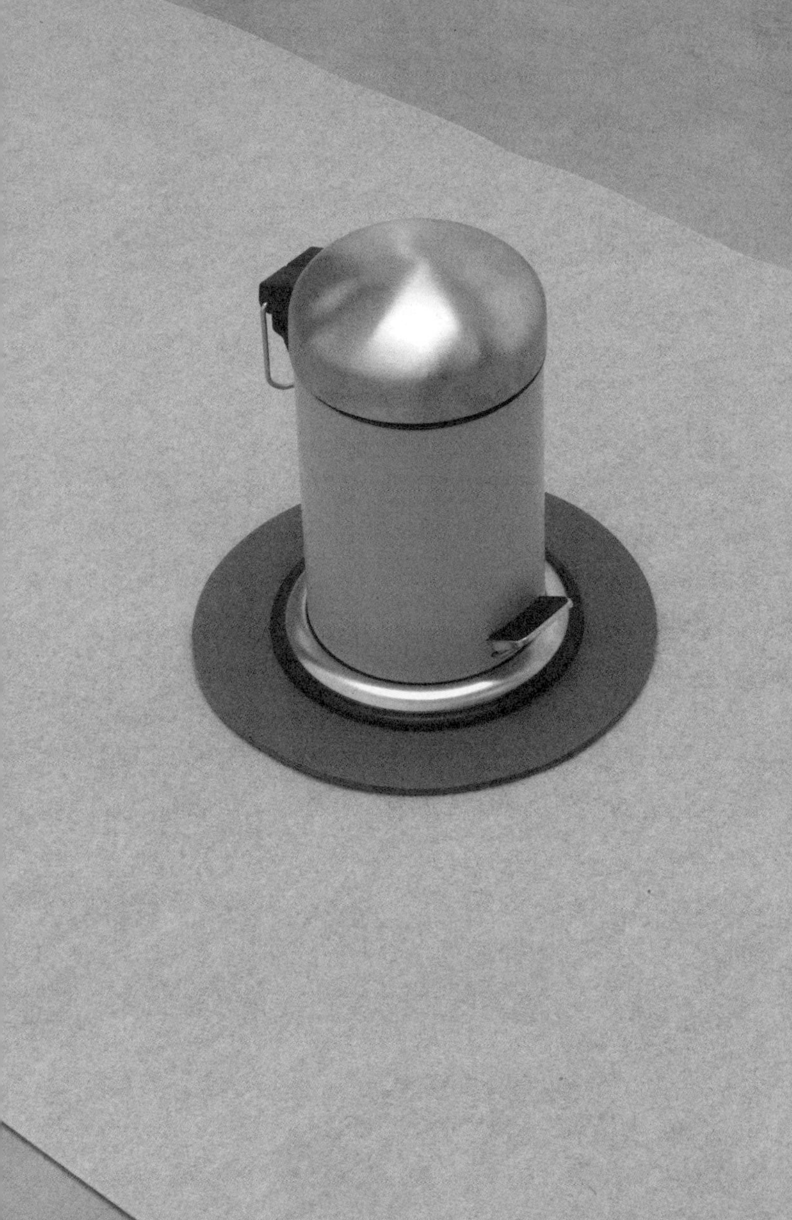

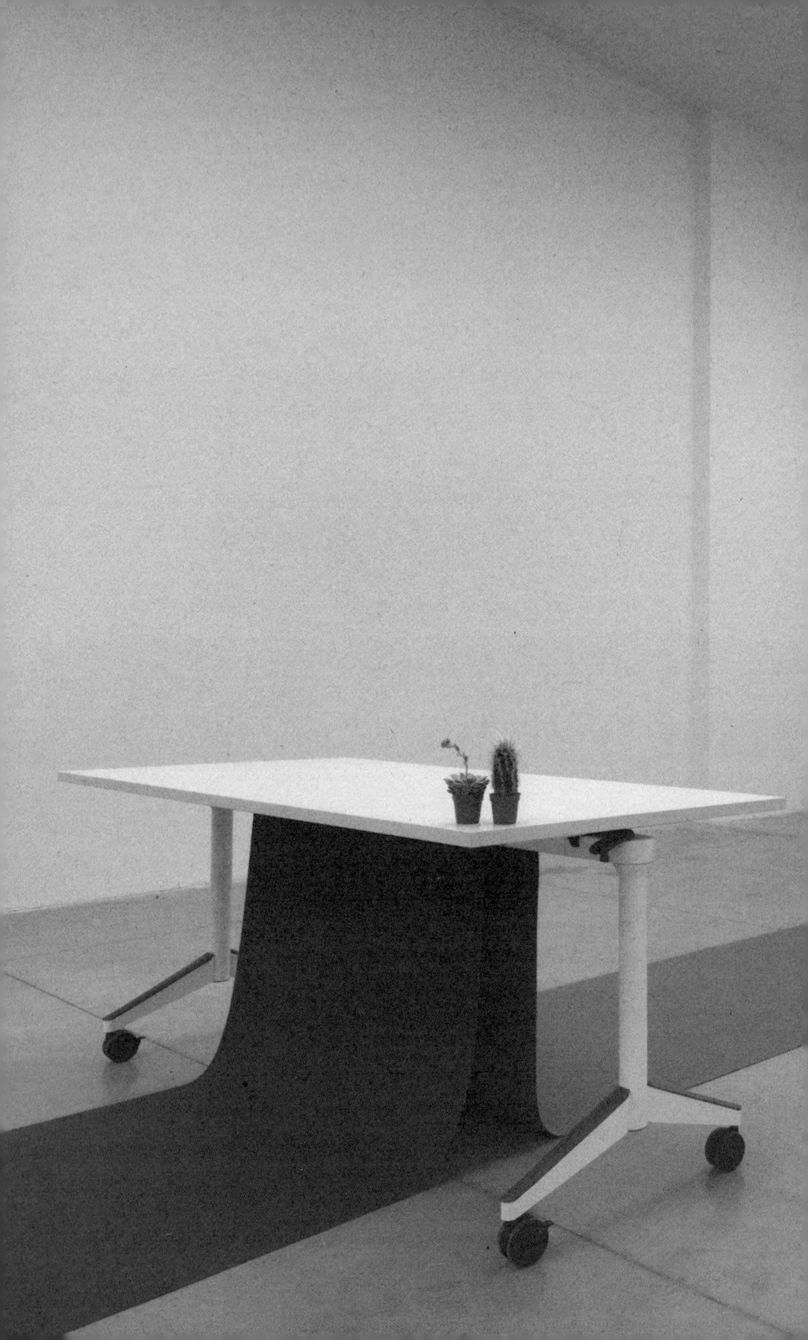

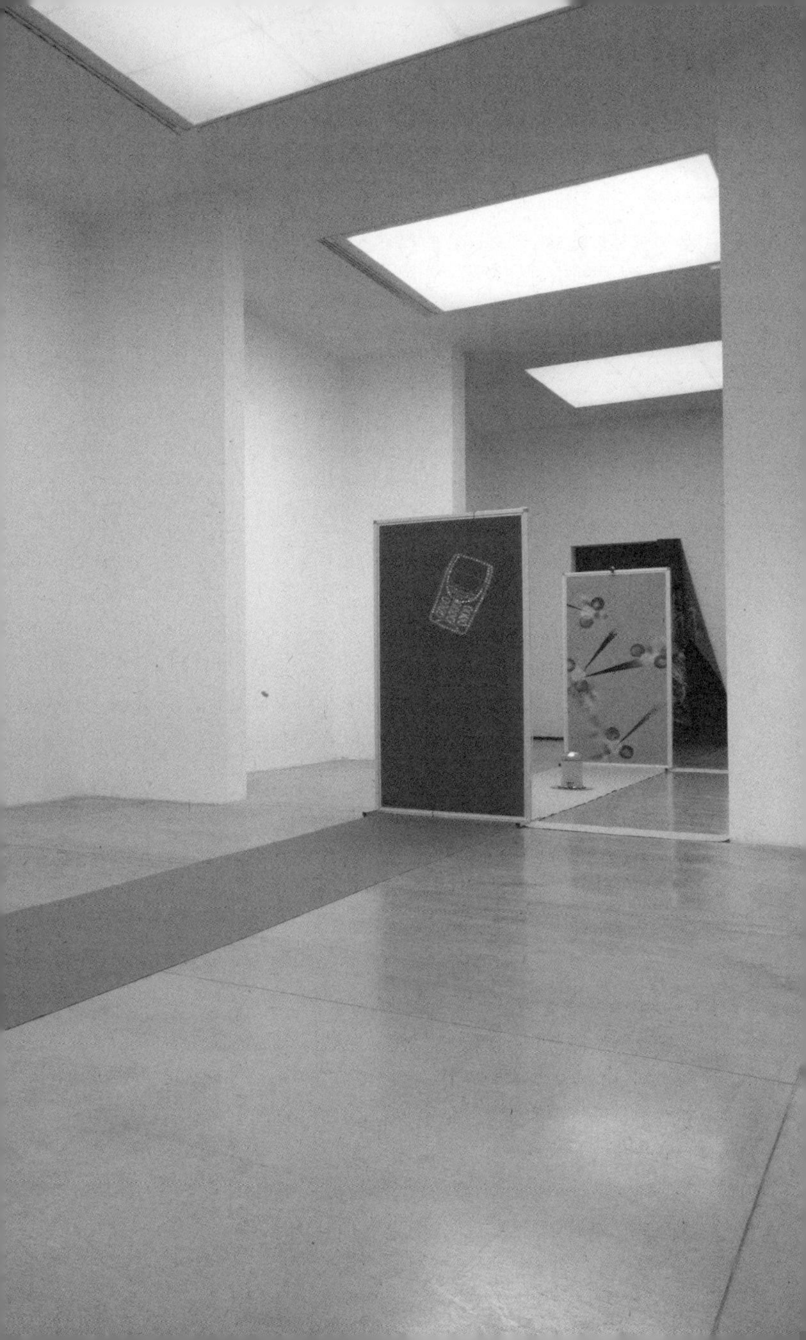

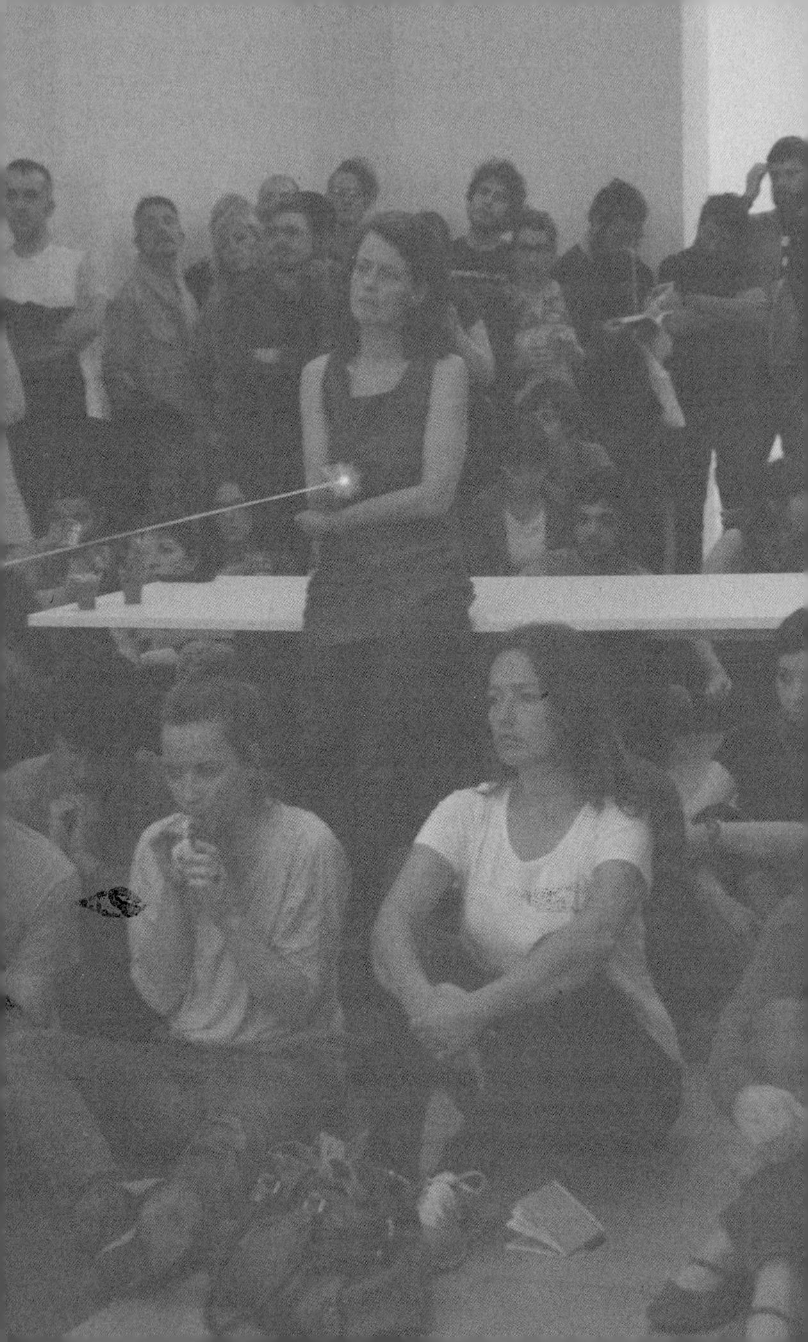

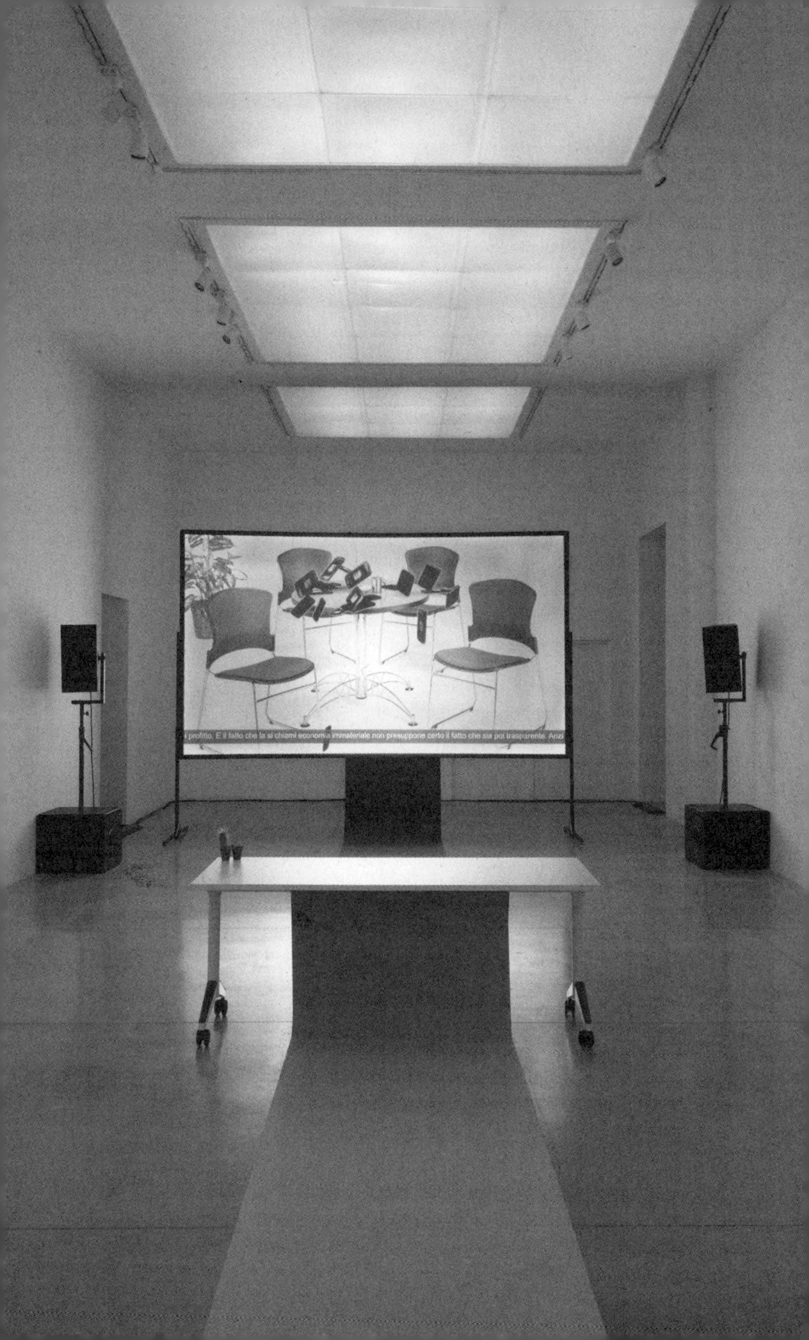
i profitto. E il fatto che la si chiami economia immateriale non presuppone certo il fatto che sia poi trasparente. Anzi

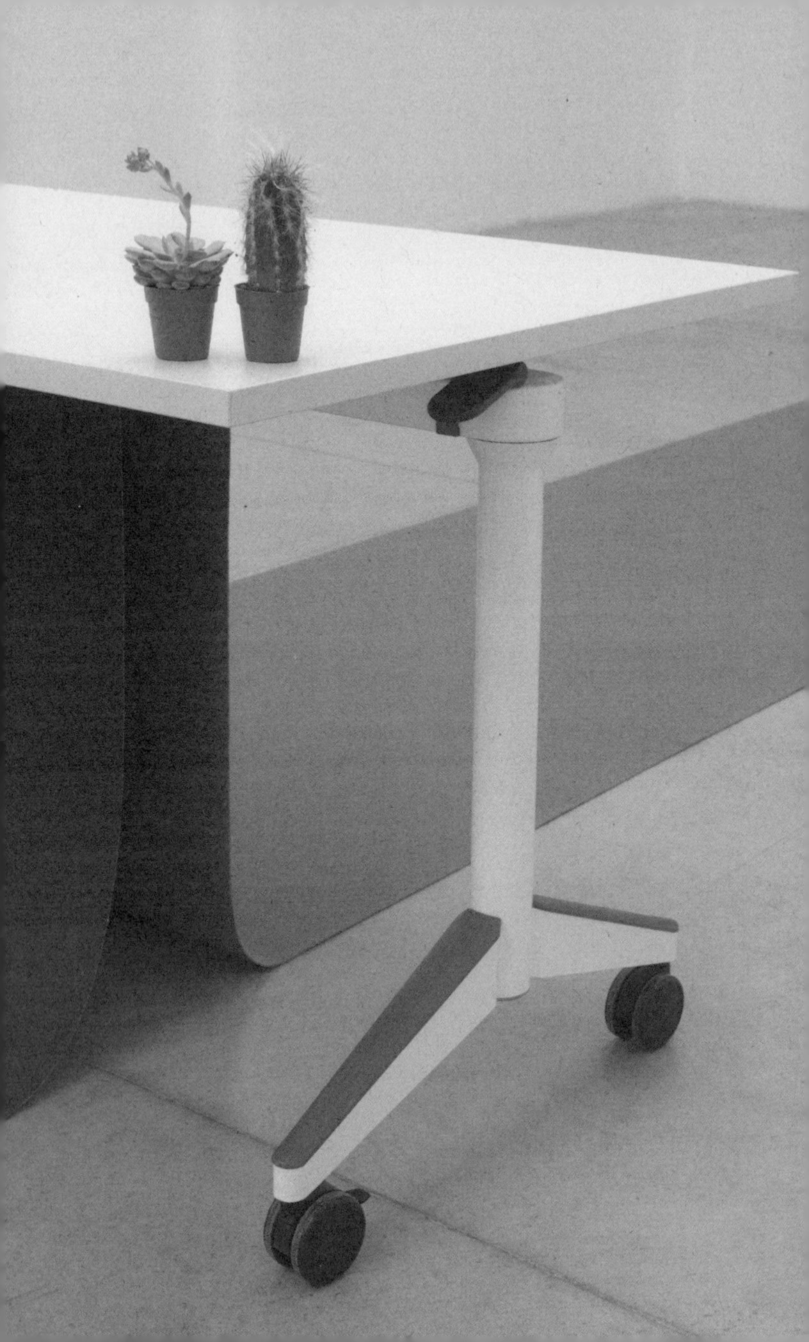

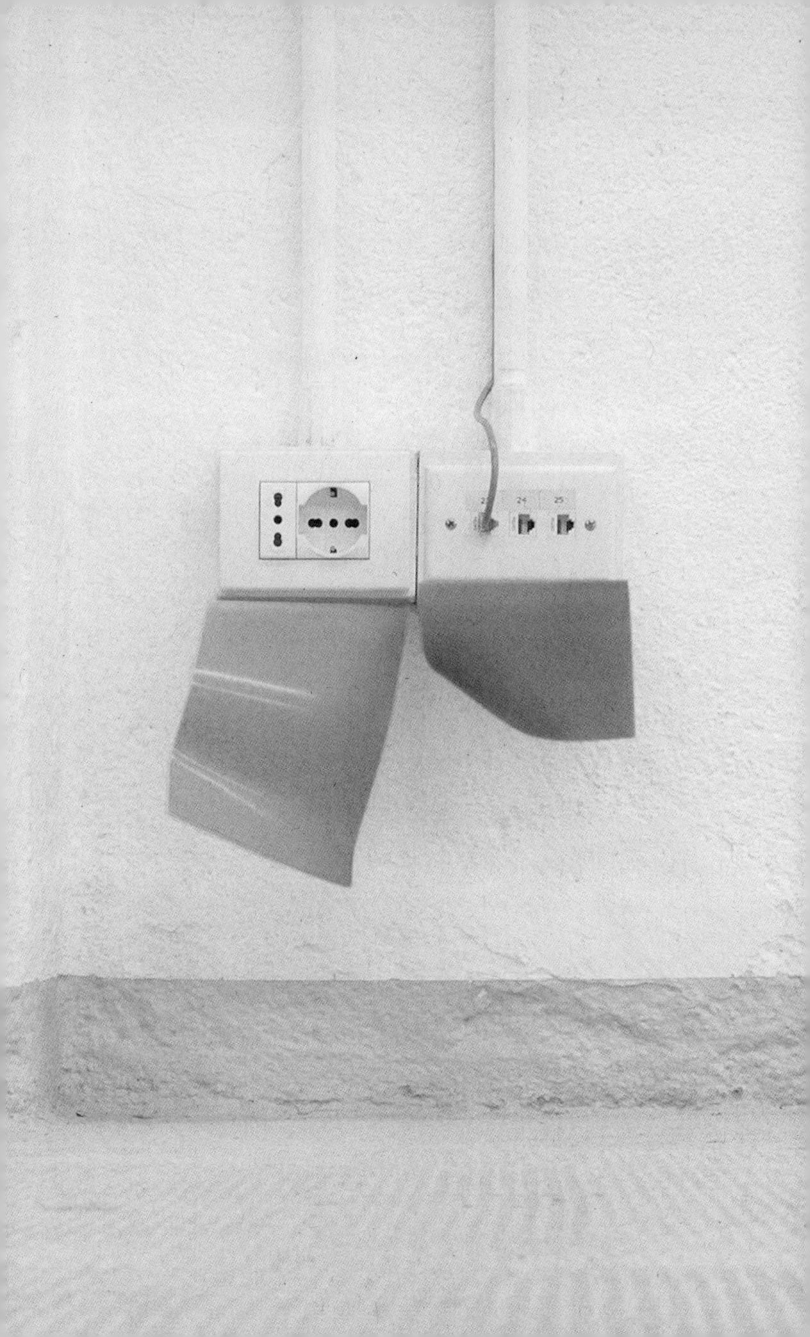

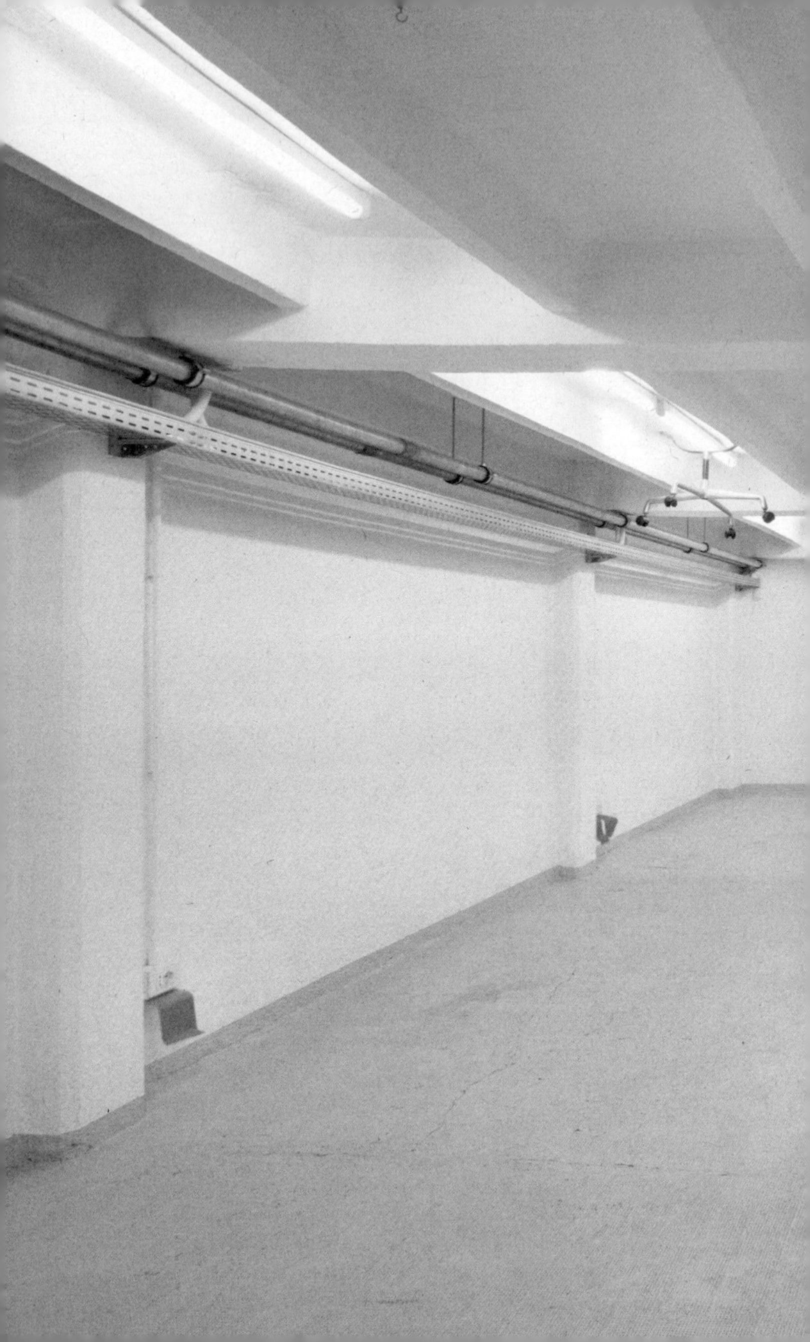

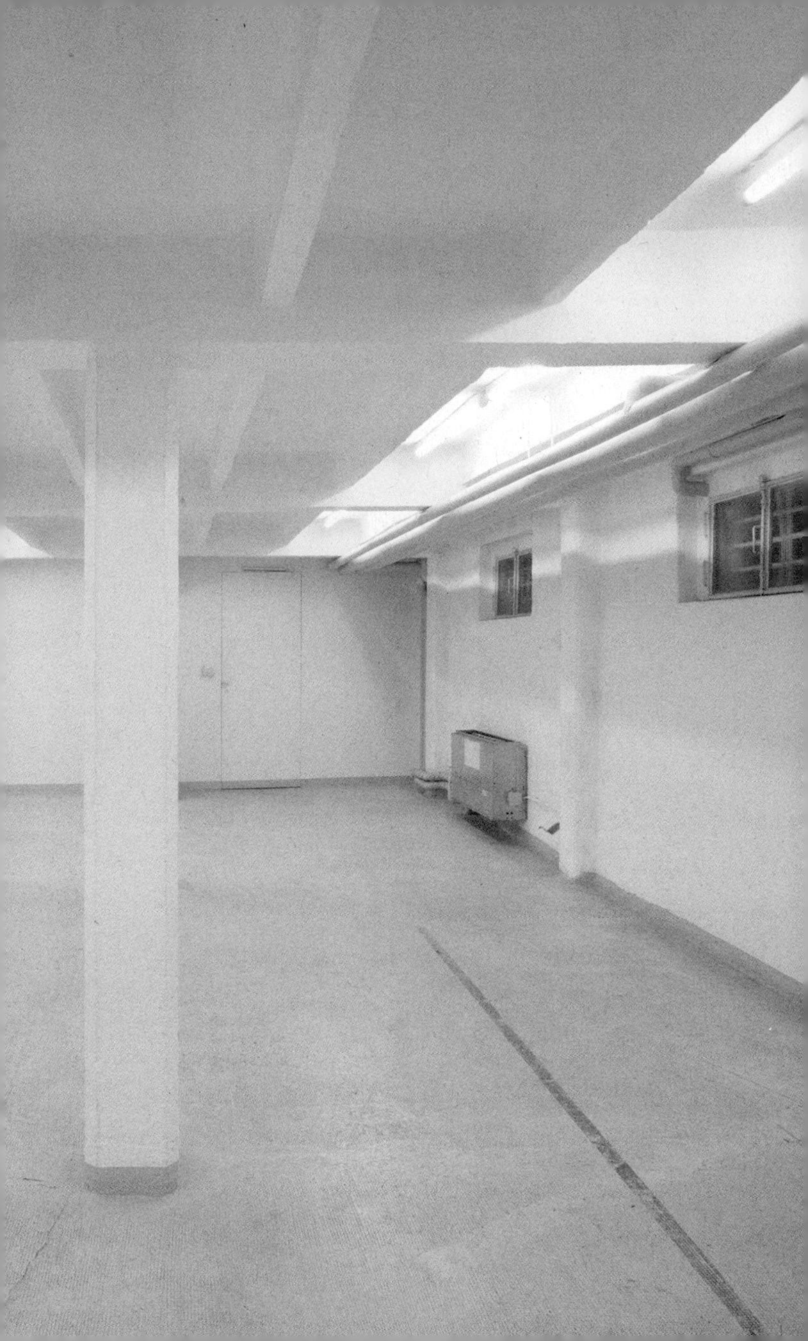

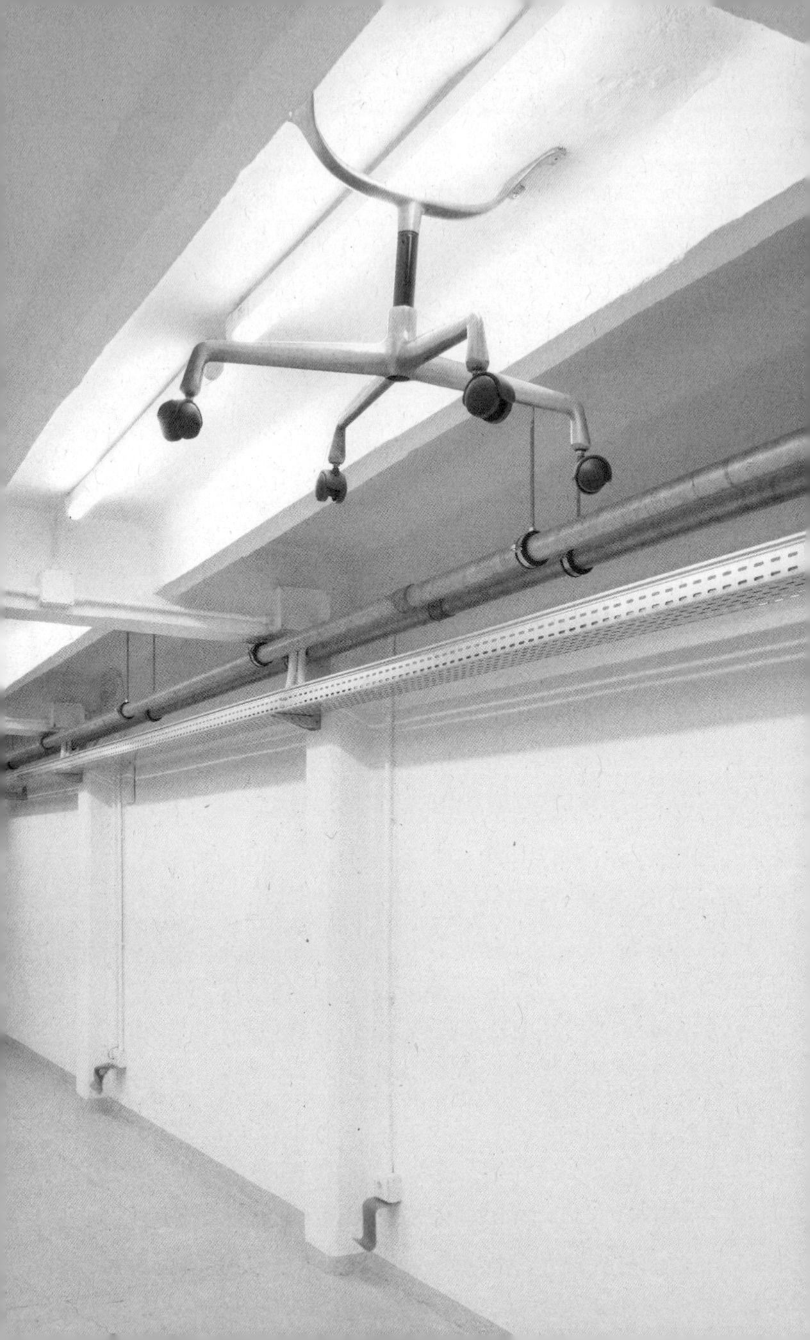

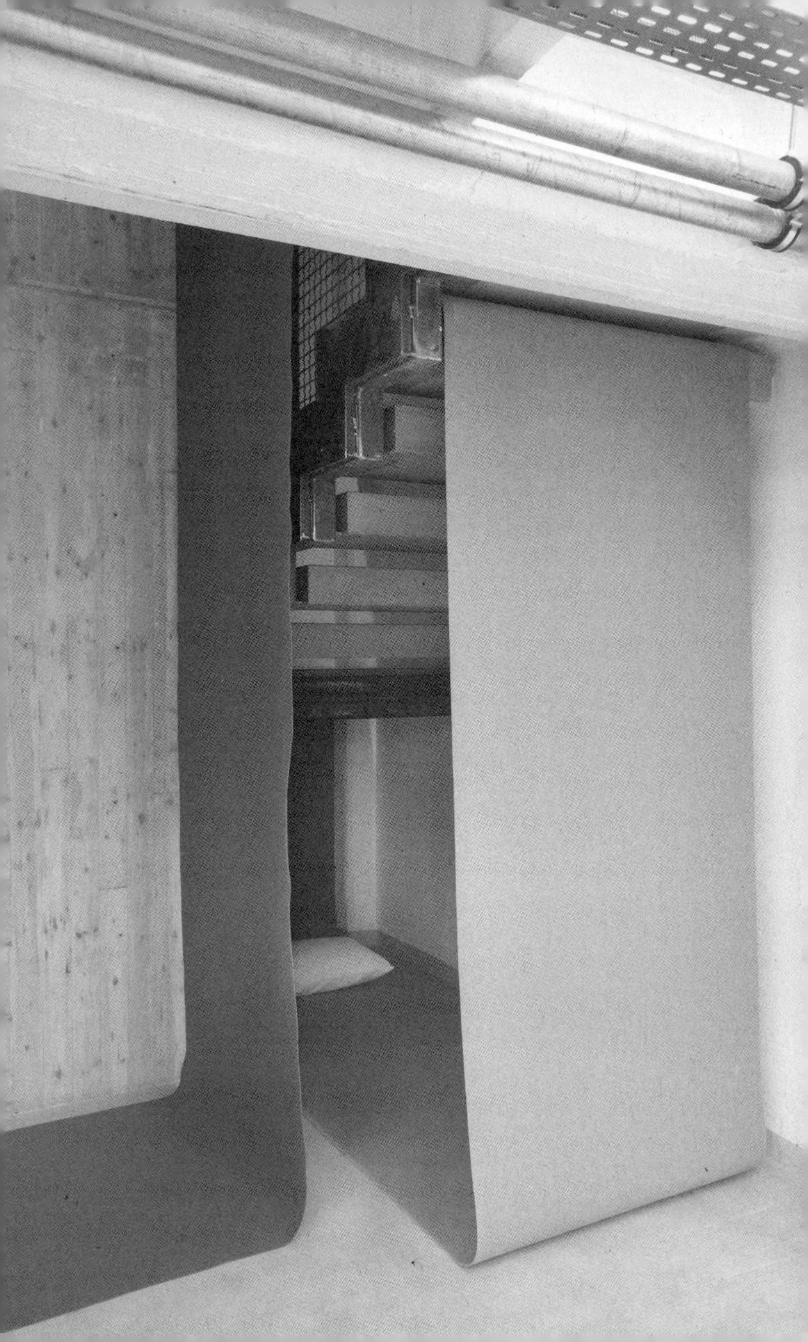

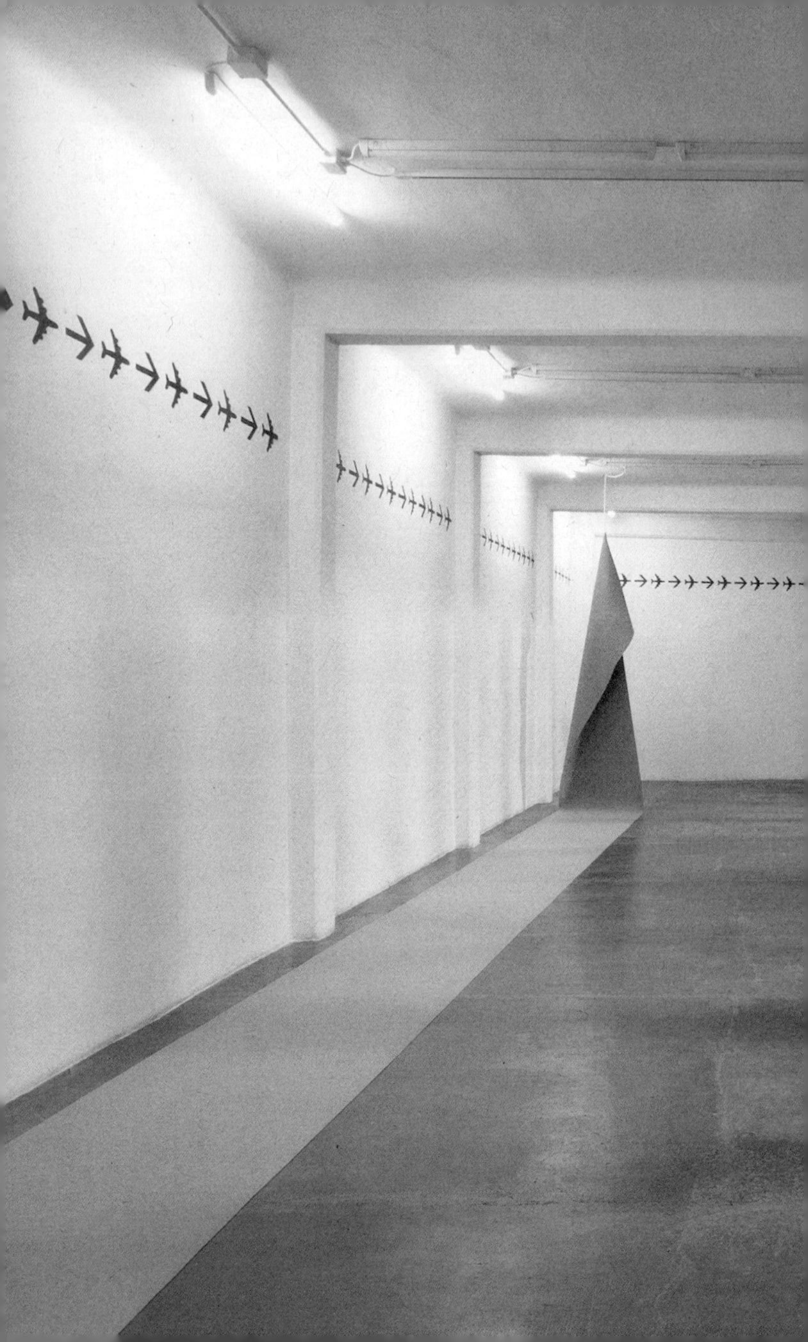

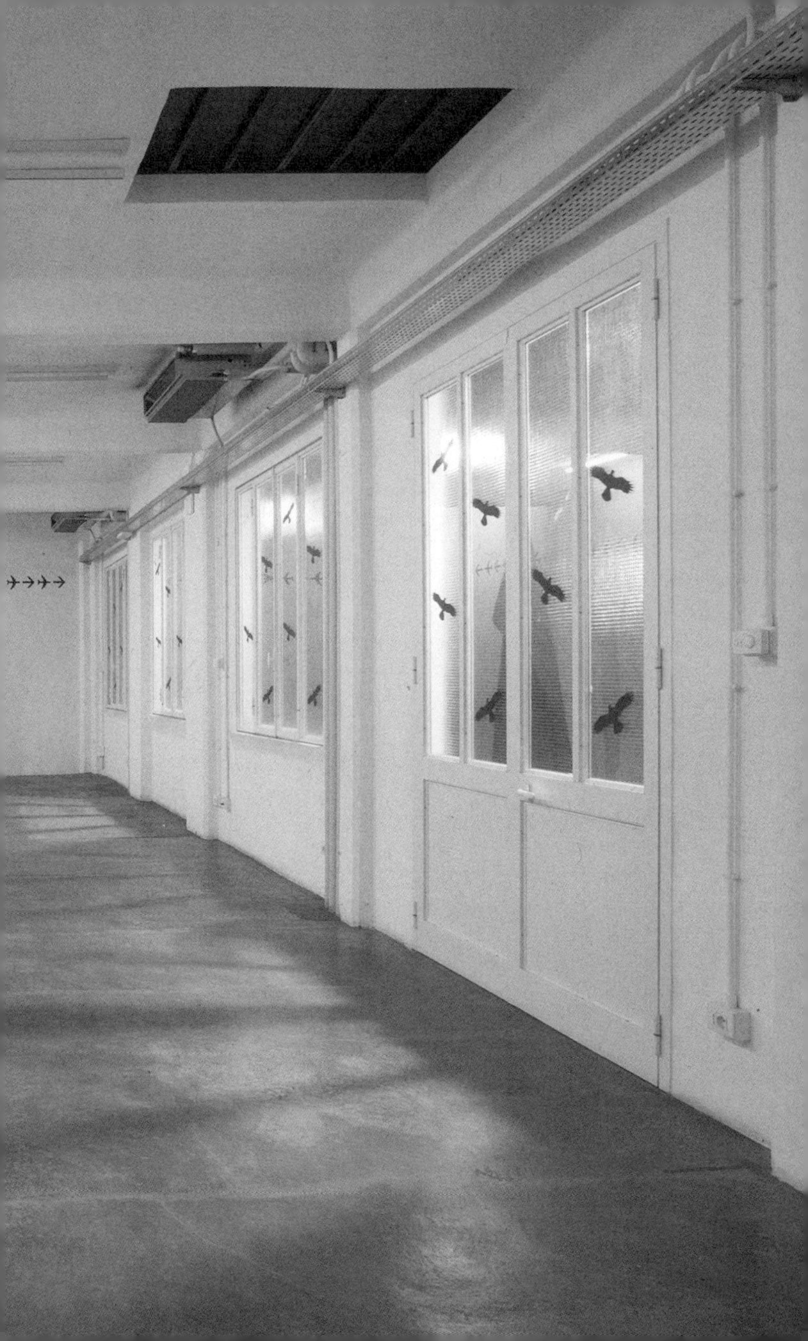

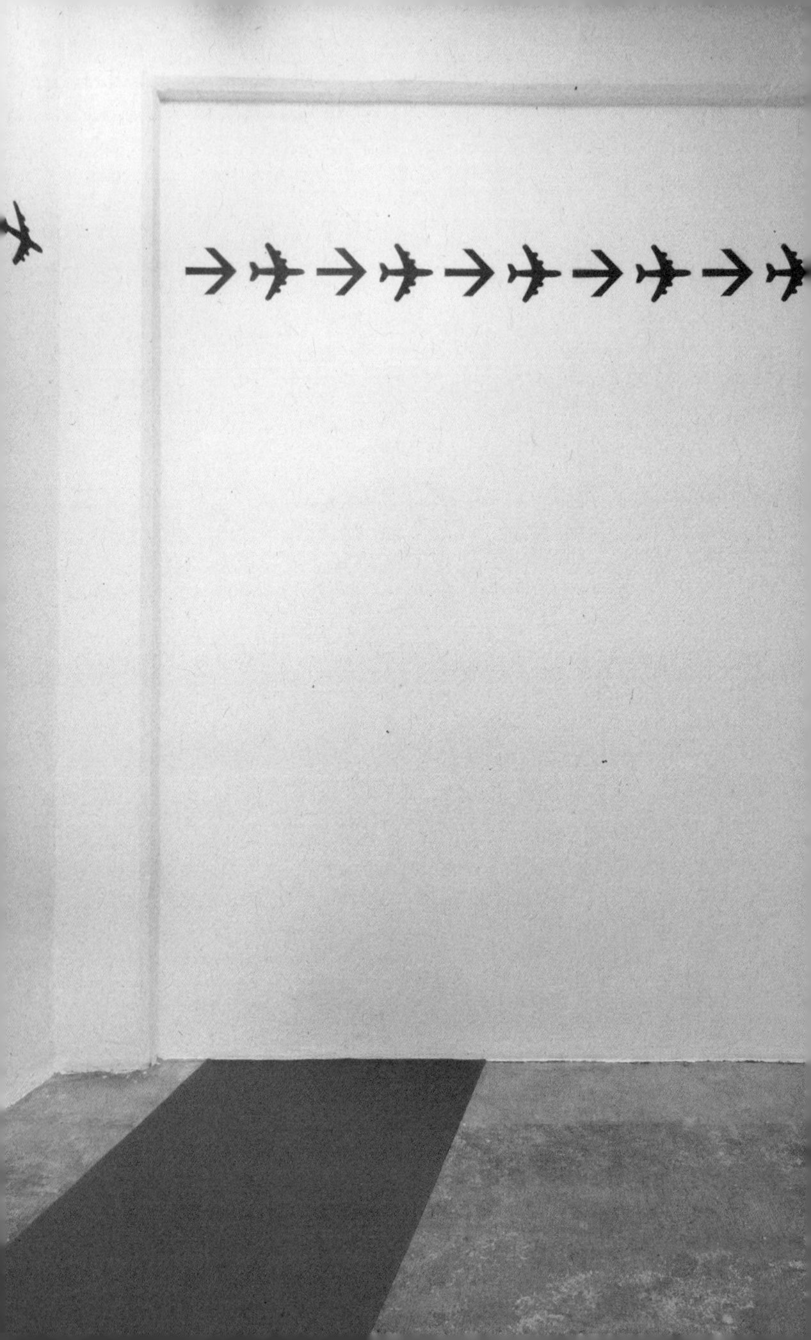

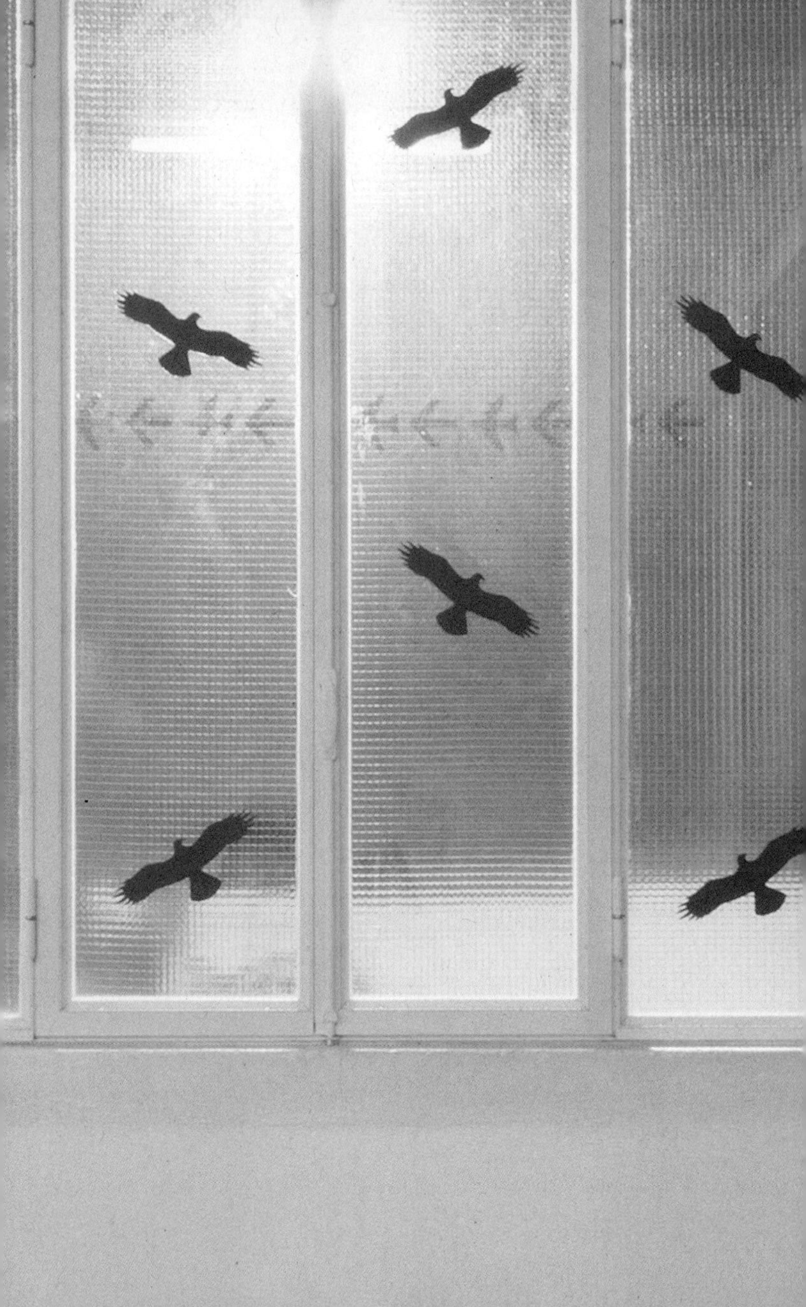

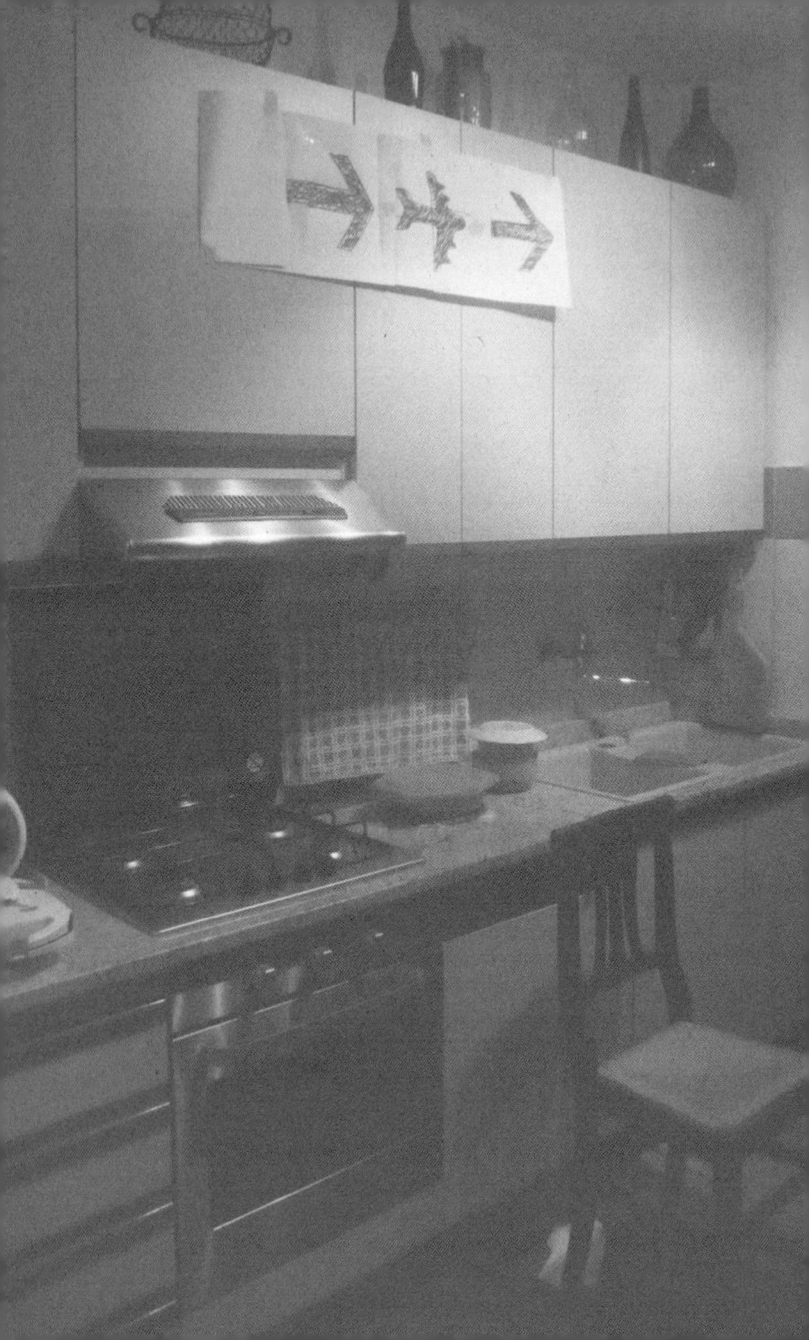

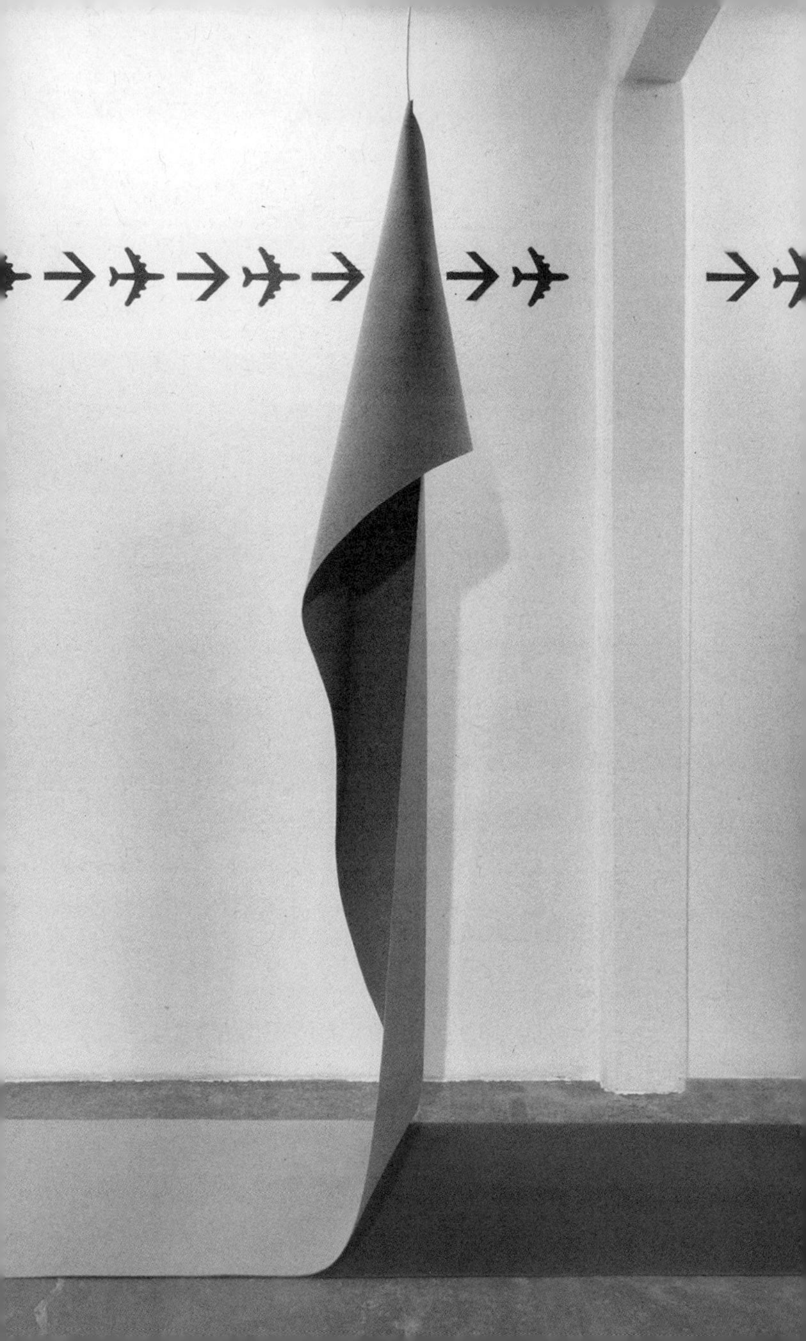

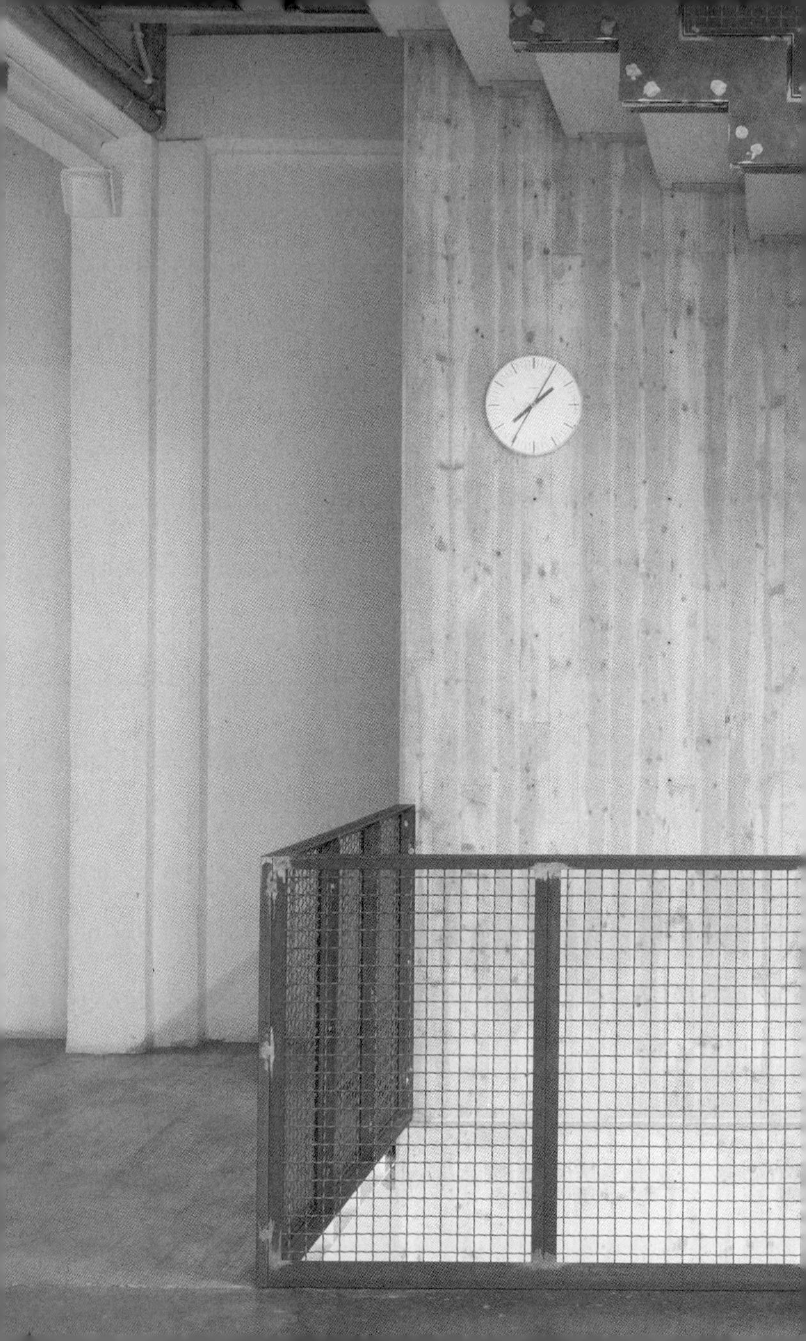

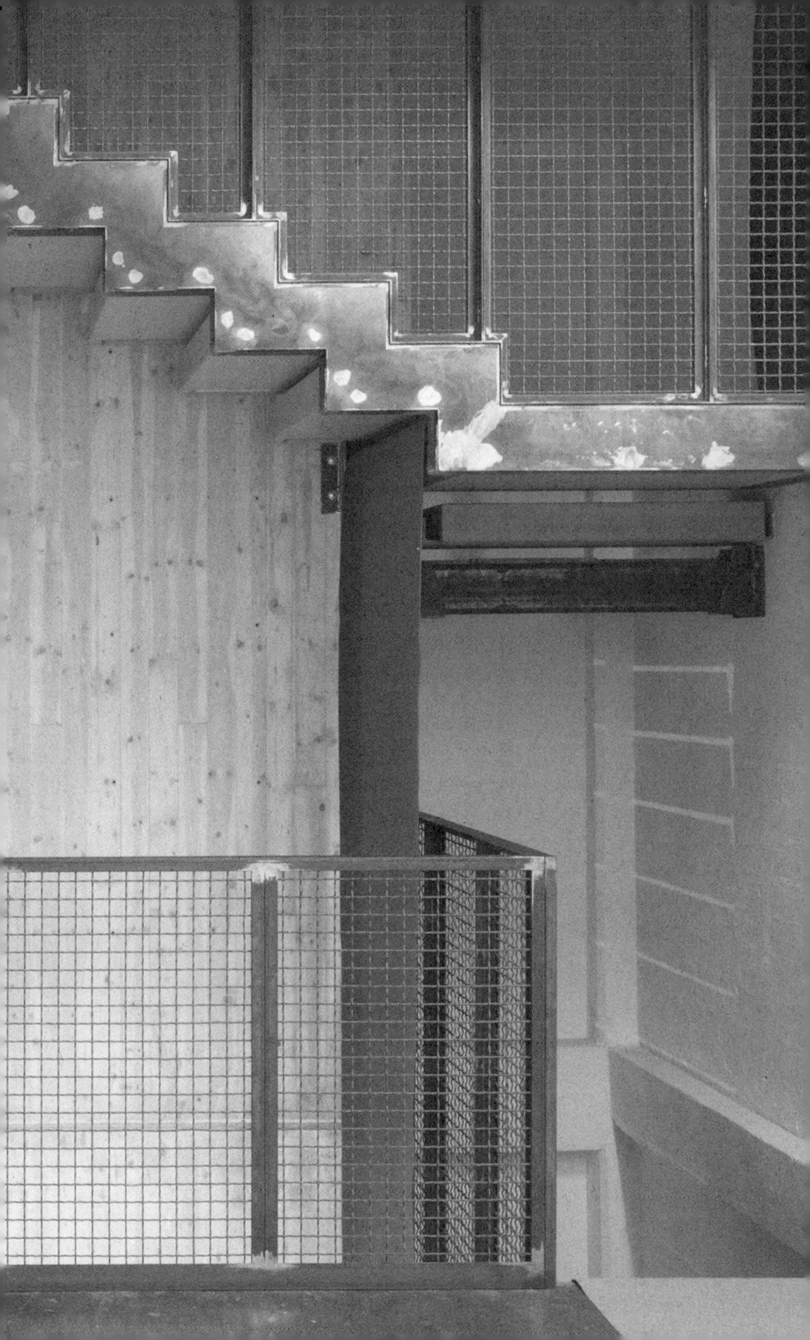

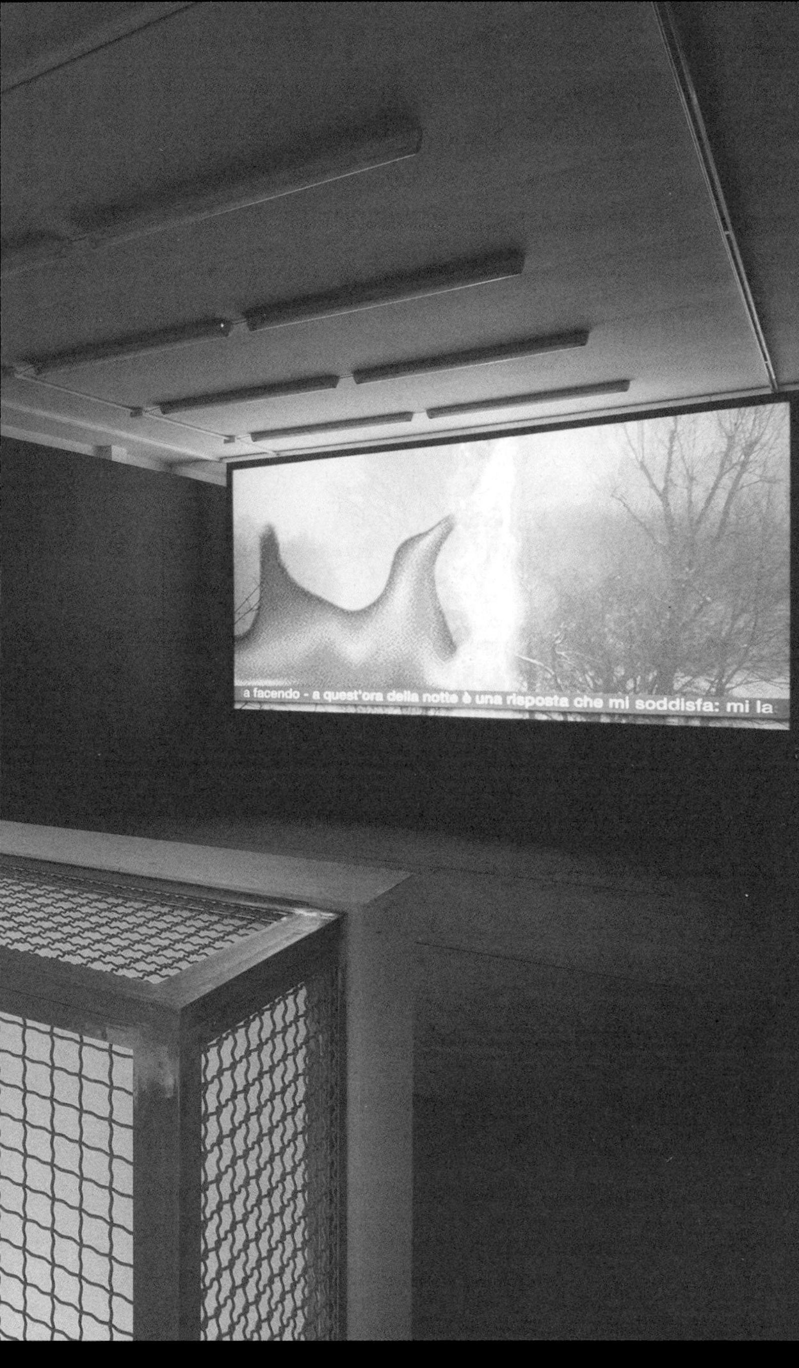
a facendo - a quest'ora della notte è una risposta che mi soddisfa: mi la

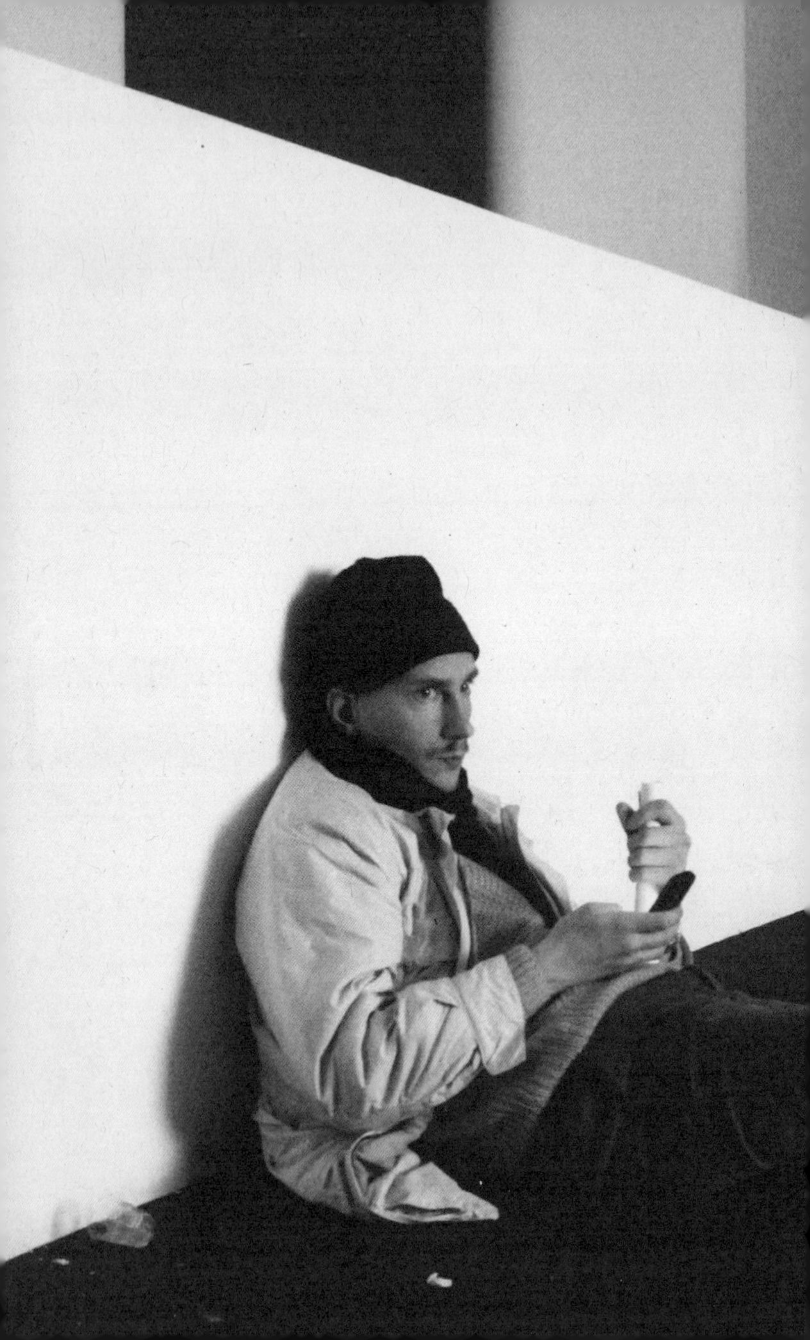

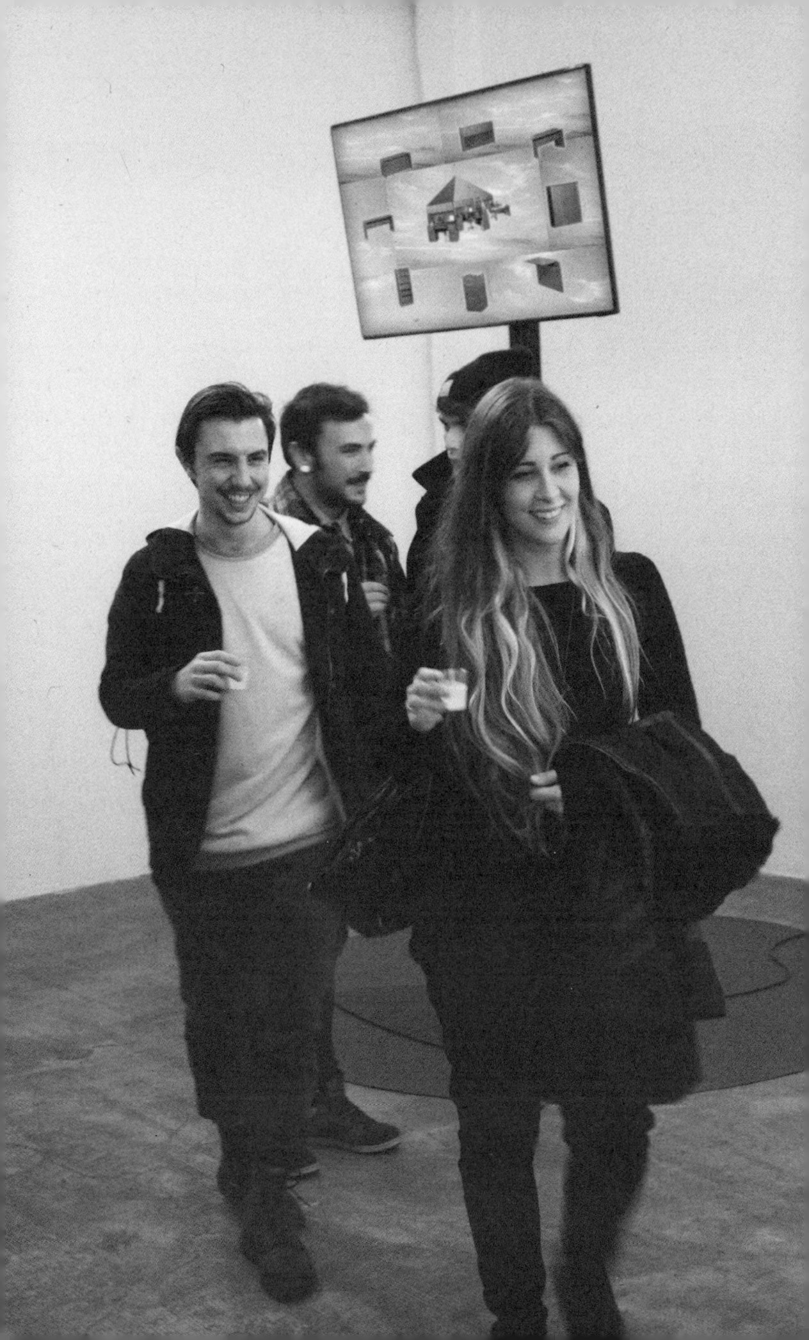

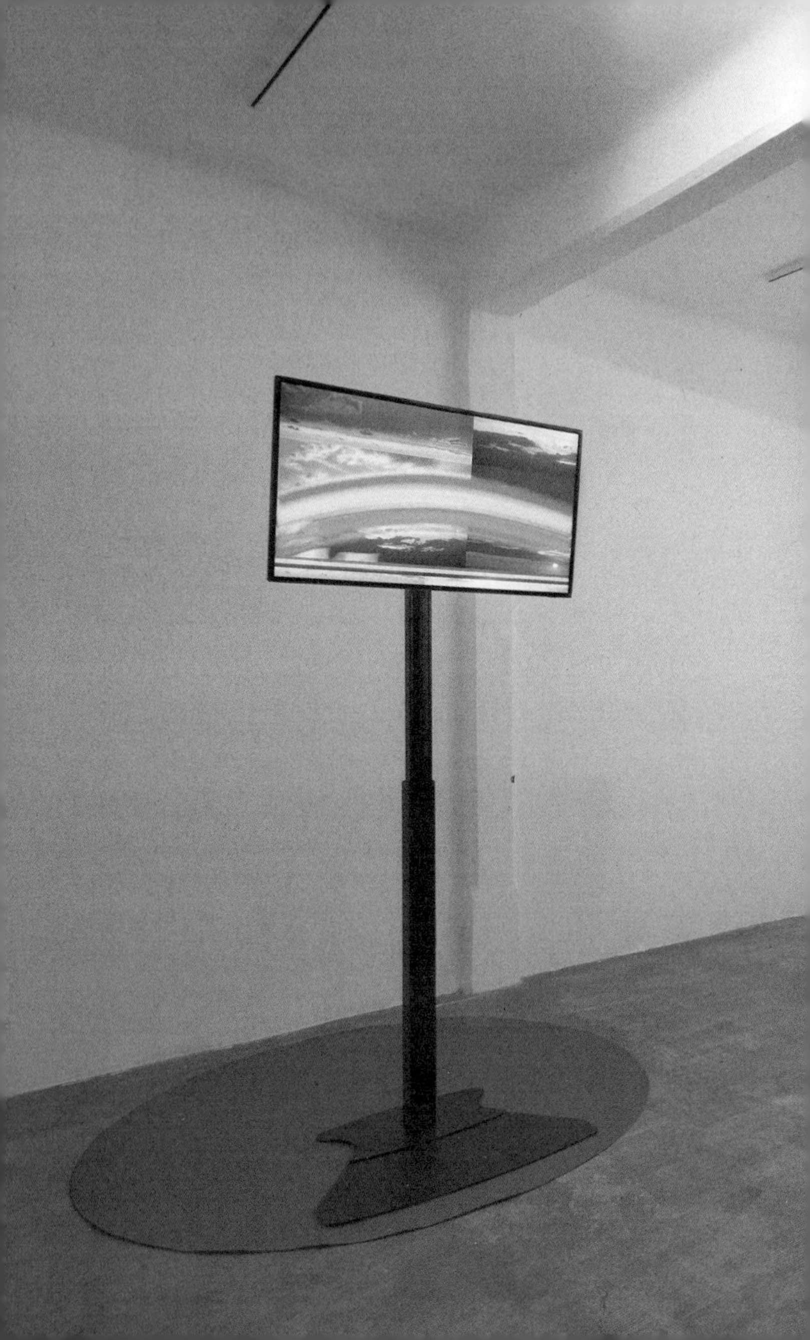

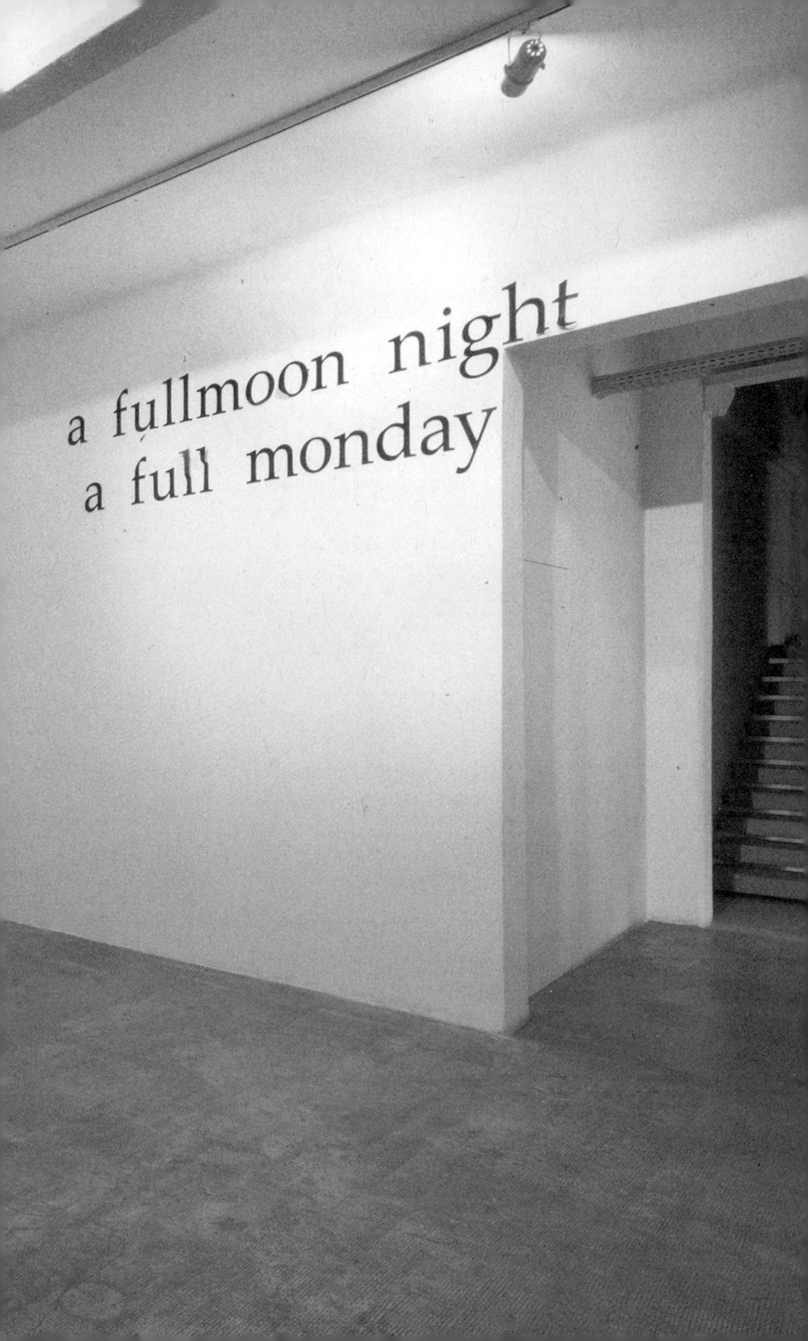

a fullmoon night
a full monday

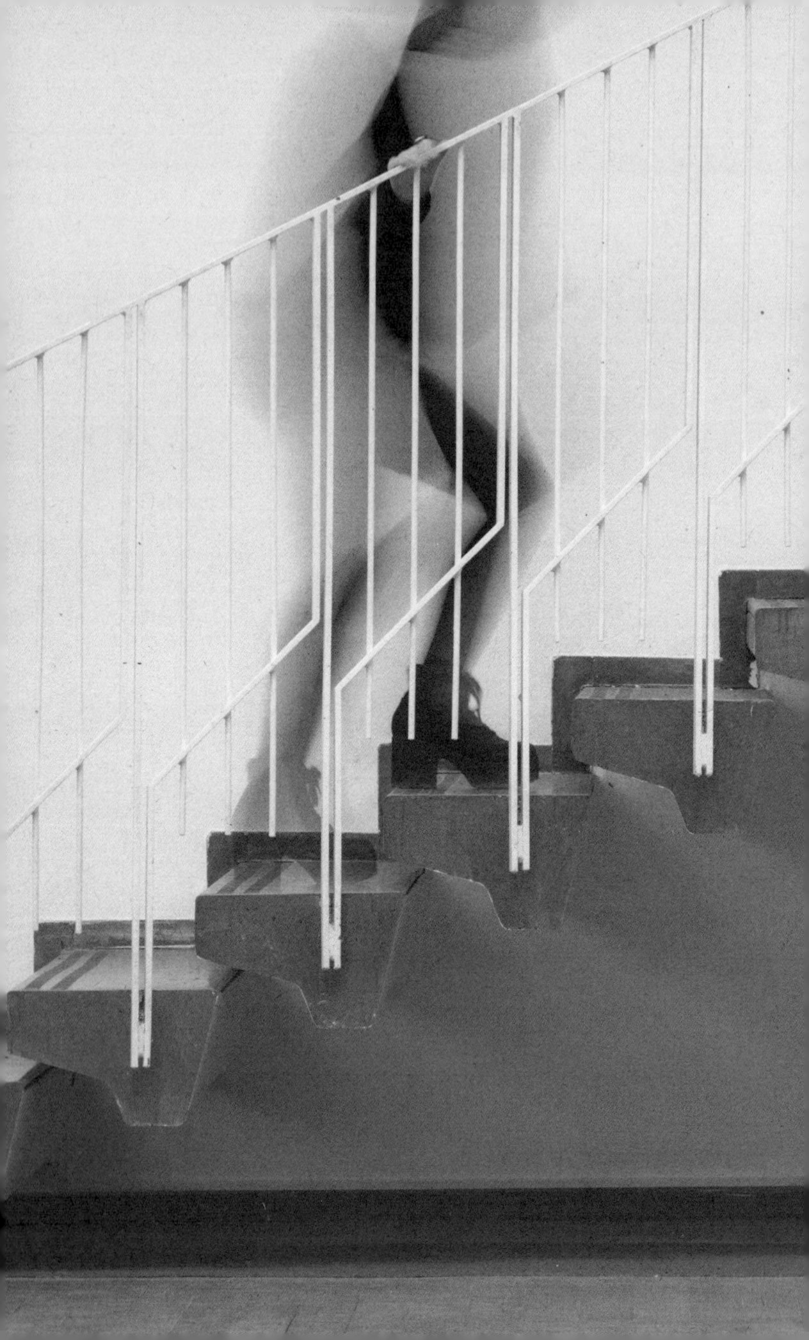

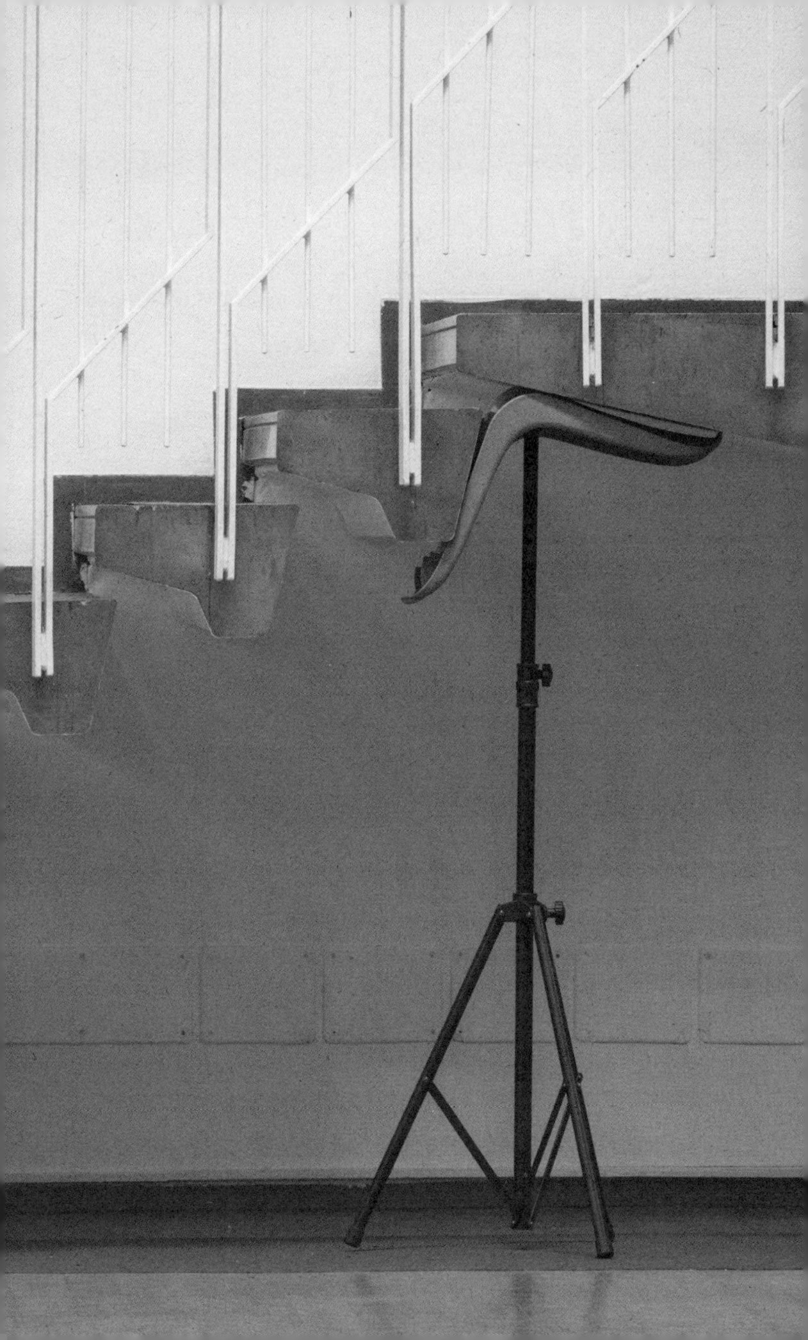

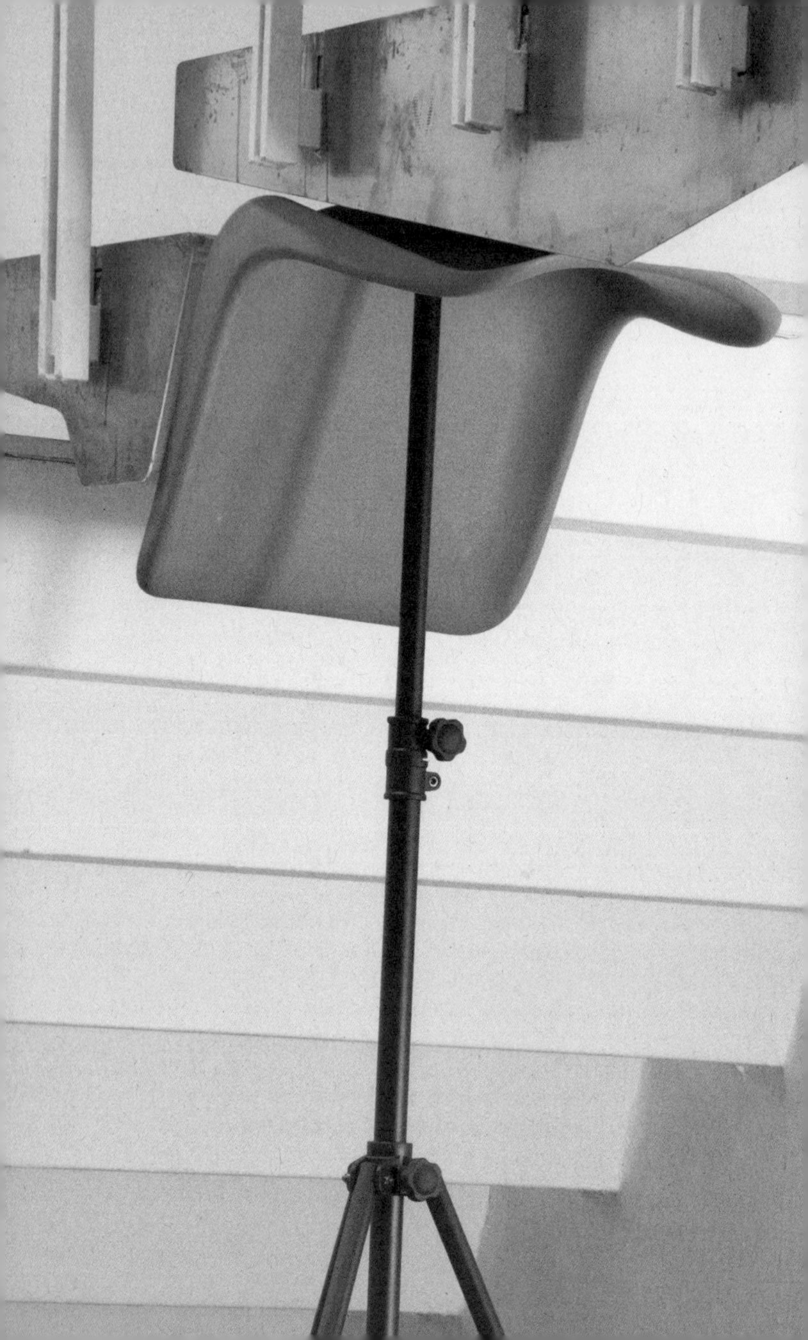

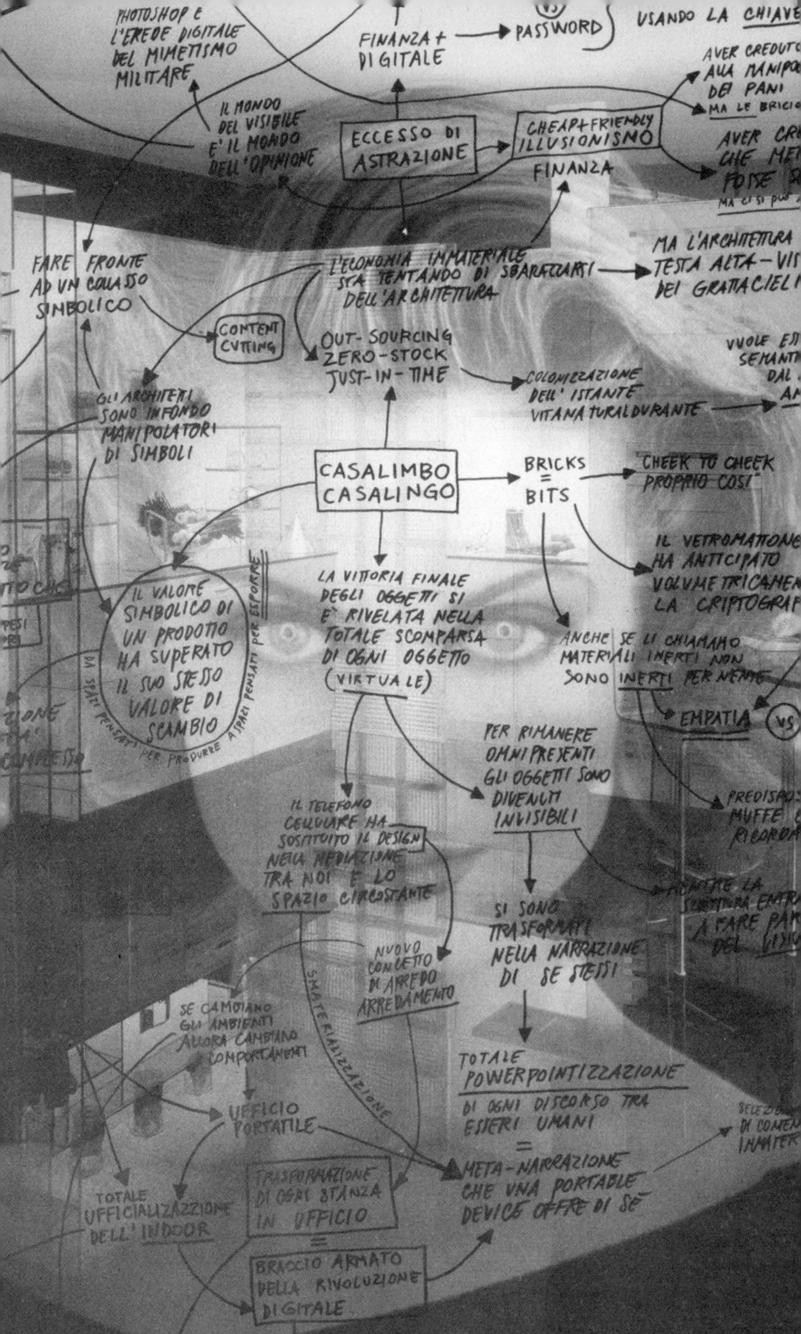

PHOTOSHOP E L'EREDE DIGITALE DEL MIMETISMO MILITARE
FINANZA + DIGITALE
PASSWORD
USANDO LA CHIAVE
AVER CREDUTO ALLA MANIPO DEI PANI MA LE BRICIO
AVER CRE CHE MEN FOSSE R MA CI SI PUO
IL MONDO DEL VISIBILE E' IL MONDO DELL'OPINIONE
ECCESSO DI ASTRAZIONE
CHEAP + FRIENDLY ILLUSIONISMO FINANZA
MA L'ARCHITETTURA TESTA ALTA — VIS DEI GRATTACIEL
FARE FRONTE AD UN COLASSO SIMBOLICO
L'ECONOMIA IMMATERIALE STA TENTANDO DI SBARAZZARSI DELL'ARCHITETTURA
CONTENT CUTTING
OUT-SOURCING ZERO-STOCK JUST-IN-TIME
COLONIZZAZIONE DELL'ISTANTE VITA NATURAL DURANTE
VUOLE ES SEMANTI DAL A
GLI ARCHITETTI SONO IN FONDO MANIPOLATORI DI SIMBOLI
CASALIMBO CASALINGO
BRICKS = BITS
CHEEK TO CHEEK PROPRIO COSI
IL VETROMATTONE HA ANTICIPATO VOLUMETRICAMEN LA CRIPTOGRAF
IL VALORE SIMBOLICO DI UN PRODOTTO HA SUPERATO IL SUO STESSO VALORE DI SCAMBIO
A SPACI PENSATI PER ESPORRE
DI SPATI PENSATI PER PRODURRE
LA VITTORIA FINALE DEGLI OGGETTI SI E' RIVELATA NELLA TOTALE SCOMPARSA DI OGNI OGGETTO (VIRTUALE)
ANCHE SE LI CHIAMANO MATERIALI INERTI NON SONO INERTI PER NIENTE
EMPATIA VS
PREDISPOS MUFFE RICORDA
PER RIMANERE OMNIPRESENTI GLI OGGETTI SONO DIVENUTI INVISIBILI
IL TELEFONO CELLULARE HA SOSTITUITO IL DESIGN NELLA MEDIAZIONE TRA NOI E LO SPAZIO CIRCOSTANTE
SMATERIALIZZAZIONE
NUOVO CONCETTO DI ARREDO ARREDAMENTO
SI SONO TRASFORMATI NELLA NARRAZIONE DI SE STESSI
A FARE PAR DEL VISIO
SE CAMBIANO GLI AMBIENTI ALLORA CAMBIANO I COMPORTAMENTI
UFFICIO PORTATILE
TOTALE POWERPOINTIZZAZIONE DI OGNI DISCORSO TRA ESSERI UMANI =
SELEZIO DI COMEN IMMATER
TOTALE UFFICIALIZZAZIONE DELL'INDOOR
TRASFORMAZIONE DI OGNI STANZA IN UFFICIO =
META-NARRAZIONE CHE UNA PORTABLE DEVICE OFFRE DI SE'
BRACCIO ARMATO DELLA RIVOLUZIONE DIGITALE

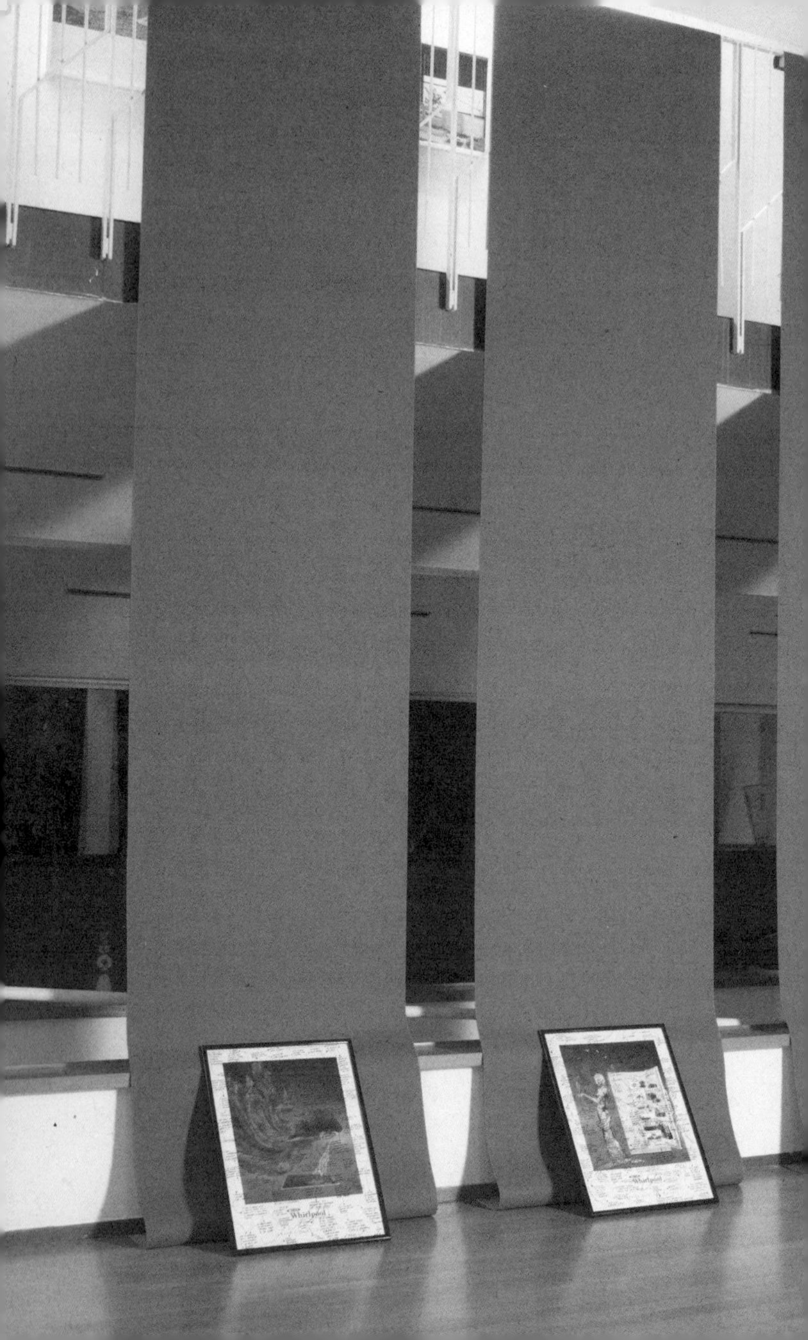

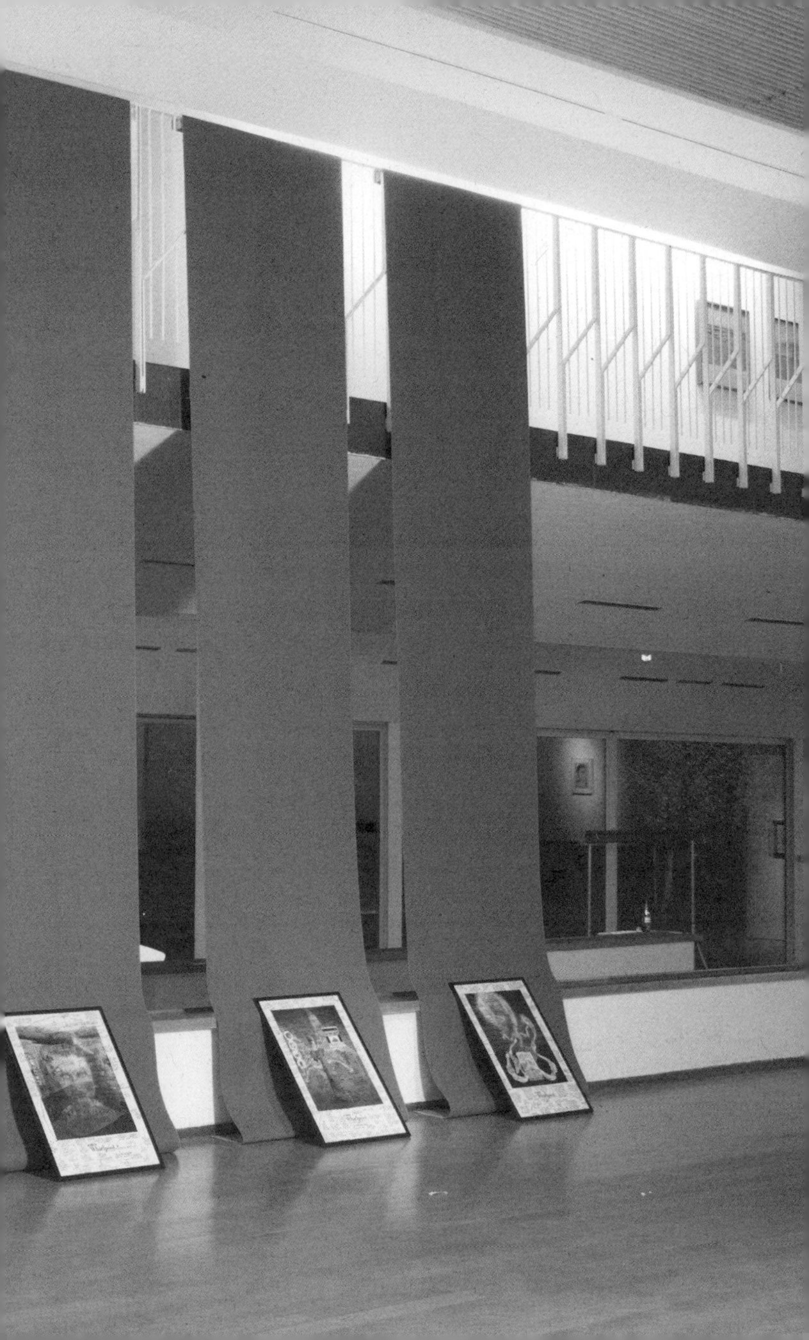

Techno Casa – an introduction to

Bricks come Bits. Proprio così: la vittoria finale degli oggetti si è rivelata nella totale scomparsa di ogni oggetto. Il telefono cellulare ha sostituito il design nella mediazione tra noi e lo spazio circostante. Tutti gli strumenti di cui ci eravamo circondati si sono smaterializzati. Per rimanere in vita – e sopravvivere al digitale – gli oggetti sono diventati invisibili, e spesso si son trasformati nella narrazione di se stessi. La totale powerpointizzazione di ogni discorso tra esseri umani – per esempio – è la meta-narrazione che un laptop offre di sé. E proprio gli esseri umani, rabdomanti di wifi, hanno permesso all'onda di propagarsi dagli oggetti ai mobili, cosicché anche l'idea stessa di arredamento si è riorganizzata. Il braccio armato della rivoluzione digitale è stato la trasformazione di ogni stanza in un ufficio – in breve: la totale ufficializzazione dell'indoor. L'arredamento modulare da ufficio, ora presente in tutto il casalimbo casalingo, ha infatti generalizzato e reso patrimonio comune la scelta della diplomazia come unico stile di vita. Ma non bisognerebbe considerare l'arredamento e l'architettura come due entità separate – anche quando si è indotti a considerare la mente e il corpo come due entità separate (e anche quando l'unica prigione che siamo in grado di accettare è quella che ognuno di noi disegna per se stesso). Anche l'architettura sta fronteggiando il digitale – certo, e lo fa a testa alta si potrebbe dire, visti i grattacieli. Tutta la nostra architettura è diventata un grande sistema di display a contenuto variabile. Questo è particolarmente evidente da Berlino, da dove sto scrivendo – osservando la Potsdamerplatzerizzazione di Schöneberg – e la trasformazione dell'aeroporto di Tempelhof in area parco destinata al bird-watching. La riconversione degli spazi ex-industriali è la scenografia di questi flashback: la vecchia industria – quella che produce oggetti materiali – si muove verso aree geografiche con manodopera a minor costo, e questi spazi qui rimasti – che un tempo erano pensati per produrre – sono diventati spazi di presentazione, esposizione e vendita. E molti musei sono parte integrante di questo processo, che inizia con l'assunzione da parte della sfera economica della narrazione creativa – e non, viceversa – da una determinazione economica dell'arte. Da quando, si potrebbe dire, il valore simbolico del prodotto

– e non il suo valore di scambio – è la fonte principale di ogni profitto. E il fatto che la si chiami economia immateriale non presuppone certo il fatto che sia poi trasparente. Anzi sta tentando visibilmente di sbarazzarsi dell'architettura, con metodi ormai consolidati come l'out-sourcing e lo zero-stock… just-in-time per la colonizzazione di ogni istante. Gli architetti sono manipolatori di simboli e l'architettura è un'interfaccia che ci chiede disperatamente contenuto: vuole essere semantizzata dal nostro amore di esseri umani. Se porgiamo attenzione, ci sono alcune superfici verticali che siamo disposti a riconoscere come muri, o pareti, a patto che offrano prese della corrente per ricaricare la batteria delle nostre interfacce portatili. E così facendo, per empatia, l'architettura sopravvive. Sopravvive grazie ai suoi materiali inerti, che inerti non son per niente anche se inerti si dice quasi sempre. La predisposizione di certi materiali ad accogliere muffe, muschi e licheni è lì a ricordarci che c'è vita nel mattone, e c'è un tipo di sudore diverso per ogni stagione.

Techno Casa – Allegato 1,12 Kb

Stavo cercando di addormentarmi, e forse ci ero anche riuscito. Dormo a molti chilometri di distanza dal mio corpo. Allontanarmi da lui richiede sempre tempo: lunghi distacchi, discorsi di commiato, saluti al giorno che se ne va applausi a quello che viene. Stavo cercando di addormentarmi, e tutto d'un tratto ho la sensazione che qualcuno mi stia puntando una luce in faccia, le palpebre sono una soglia molto sottile, la mente finge di essere impegnata su altro. Mi riavvicino di corsa al mio corpo per svegliarmi di soprassalto. Non riesco veramente a spiegarmi che cosa stia succedendo, controllo sommariamente ma in casa non c'è nessuno. Fuori dalla finestra forse la tempesta. Mi metto quieto e risuccede di nuovo – qualcuno mi punta una luce in faccia e questa volta è proprio chiaro: si fa strada un leggero presentimento, un brivido di assoluta desolazione, l'idea di esseri soli e minuscoli ma in forma di sensazione. Alzo la testa dal cuscino e cerco un elicottero fra le nuvole, una macchina volante ripescata nelle mie fantasie, ma ristrutturate e aumentate dalla fiction. E questi pensieri sono accompagnati dal boato di un tuono, colonna sonora per un'apocalisse personale fra le lenzuola. Proprio il suono mi fa capire che non si trattava altro che di un lampo. Nonostante mi risulti abbastanza incomprensibile come un lampo possa essere arrivato ai miei occhi senza bruciare niente strada facendo – a quest'ora della notte è una risposta che mi soddisfa: mi lascio abbracciare dalla rivelazione sonora in assenza di prove scientifiche, e torno immediatamente ad appisolarmi. Adesso che è evidente, la tempesta fuori dalla finestra mi accompagna dolcemente. E al risveglio, rintronato, ho raccontato a M. quello che mi è successo – ma non avevo prove condivisibili – solo flash di luce coadiuvati da parole. Poi giorni dopo un giorno di sole: ero alla finestra per dare senso al vuoto causato dal repentino cambio di stagione. Avvicinandomi alle finestre penso a quello che mi raccontano altri delle loro finestre, di questi momenti in cui il mondo è comprensibile perché inserito nella cornice lignea che ne isola dei frammenti. O nella cornice del display, del monitor, del touch screen – ma questa è un'altra storia. Ora mi torna in mente quello che mi ha raccontato A. che abita vicino alla Stazione Centrale di Milano, e dalla sua finestra – se non ricordo male – ha seguito dall'alto – passo dopo passo – un uomo che si stava costruendo la sua architettura informale: una casa in strada. E questo mi porta subito a Napoli, lungo il mare. Stavo aspettando che C. mi venisse a prendere in macchina, e riempivo il suo ritardo osservando una tenda da campeggio posizionata su un marciapiede, circondata da cani che dormivano. Un uomo ben vestito nel frattempo arriva con una busta della spesa e si china ad accarezzare sulla testa tutti i cani, uno a uno, si abbassa verso il marciapiede in maniera ritmica a seconda della stazza dell'animale che accarezza. Poi chiama in direzione della tenda, e lo fa ripetutamente finché qualcuno da dentro non risponde. Hanno un breve scambio vocale che alle mie orecchie giunge senza consonanti. Poi l'uomo lascia lì la busta e se ne va, sento il suono inconfondibile della chiusura lampo della tenda ma non vedo cosa succede perché C. è arrivato – forse da un po' – e mi ha visto lì impalato, e ora mi acceca ripetutamente con i fari abbaglianti del suo veicolo. La luce si intromette tra il mio sguardo e la tenda perché rimbalza sulla vetrina di una banca. E forse non in quell'attimo, ma in questo preciso istante ho trovato una soluzione. Una volta S. mi ha raccontato che quel palazzo molto alto che è vicino alla Stazione Centrale di Milano causa problemi ai palazzi più bassi e più anziani che vi sorgono attorno. Essendo il grattacielo rivestito da finestre specchianti – nei giorni di sole i raggi rimbalzano contro di lui e vanno a sbattere sulle altre architetture lì attorno, corrodendone gli infissi lignei delle finestre e le imposte. Questi raggi – che arrivano più o meno sparsi – vengono raggruppati dalle finestre specchianti del grattacielo e rispediti in direzioni ben precise, ad umani che non li han chiesti ma forse ci si abbronzano. Ecco come il lampo è arrivato ai miei occhi quella notte: anche davanti alle mie finestre sorgono specchi verticali che sfidano le nuvole e moltiplicano la città. I cartelli turistici che raccontano la storia dei grattacieli ai passanti rivelano: FROM A GRAND HOTEL TO AN OFFICE BLOCK. Grattacieli che hanno la pelle lucida, come la mia durante il sonno. Un lampo rispedito da un'architettura consenziente – che riorganizza i moti turbinosi del cielo in maniera distratta ma tecnicamente perfetta – e fa da tramite tra me, il mio sonno, e l'imprevisto delle stelle. E forse, se ogni grattacielo è un faro part-time, allora questa non è la fine della Storia, ma è la fine della Geografia.

Techno Casa – Allegato 3,19 Kb

L'insegnate stava illustrando alcune idee relative al packaging degli oggetti. Ci faceva capire che il motivo per cui non c'è stata alcuna innovazione grafica di rilievo sulla costa dei libri, è che nella vetrina dei negozi i libri vengono esposti di faccia – e non di fianco. Camminando per strada, davanti alle vetrine delle librerie, mi stupivo della tendenza a esporre ripetutamente una di fianco all'altra molte copie della stessa pubblicazione – spesso una novità fresca di stampa. Più il libro era tascabile e più era necessario moltiplicarlo per venderlo, e si costruiva così l'insegna variabile di un negozio che – apparentemente – vendeva un unico prodotto. Questo mi riporta a quello strano fenomeno del contrappasso – per il quale si finisce a comprare molti libri proprio quando non si ha il tempo di leggerli. Così facendo – ci si regala una possibilità in divenire, ci si asseconda onestamente – ripromettendosi di es-

sere migliori. Il libro – nel momento del suo acquisto – è la manifestazione spazio-temporale di
un nostro essere al mondo al quale tendiamo per
natura. Quando finalmente troveremo il tempo
di leggerlo – saremo nel frattempo cambiati – ma
avremo fisicamente edificato una parte di noi che
ci è appartenuta. Infatti – come mi ha fatto notare
L. – si è portati a considerare l'acquisto di un libro
come un gesto eticamente corretto anche quando
(per necessità o virtù) si è ormai messa completamente in discussione l'idea stessa di consumo
(acquisto di soluzioni). E quindi poi finisce che
i libri diventano parte del design delle nostre
stanze – si accumulano ricordandoci una parte di
noi pronta ad essere risvegliata da un momento
all'altro. Oppure si sovrappongono verticalizzando la linea del tempo – e aumentano la volumetria del nostro mobilio. I libri, si potrebbe dire,
danno un senso all'arredamento – danno agio alla
sua modularità composta da superfici orizzontali
in perenne attesa. E pensare che questo avviene
in un periodo storico in cui l'editoria è messa in
discussione dalla rivoluzione digitale – e leggere su carta si sta dimostrando essere sempre di
più un lusso sopraffino. Forse il libro è un gesto
che difende l'architettura: il suo essere al mondo
è una naturale risemantizzazione di ogni stanza.
Se ogni libro è un gesto che difende l'architettura – allora mi è ancora più chiaro comprendere
il motivo per il quale la scrittura è diventata una

pratica estesa nell'arte contemporanea: noi artisti siamo impegnati a difendere il nostro posto di lavoro – e prevenire una sua definitiva scomparsa. La dissoluzione dell'architettura, infatti – una sua mimetizzazione col mondo di simboli circostanti – toglierebbe all'artista il cosiddetto luogo deputato, quello che da senso, si potrebbe dire, al suo operato. Come chiudere la fabbrica a un operaio – e far sì che quel luogo diventi una sfumatura di un mondo che è stato, o meglio, la proiezione di un essere umano in pace con le macchine che sarebbe anche potuto essere. Ma il fatto che gli artisti oggi scrivano di più significa che sono più coscienti del loro ruolo all'interno della società oppure – come mi ha fatto notare F. – che le loro pratiche siano sempre meno effettive – e quindi la scrittura è sinonimo di frustrazione? Lacrime grammatiche e l'annichilimento della vita nel discorso. Ma se c'è la voglia si esce, se non c'è la voglia si scrive (o dipinge) – il fine ultimo (volente o nolente) è incontrare i propri simili. E non è vero che oggi si scrive di più perché scrivere non costa niente – scrivere costa vivere – e quindi non costa niente nemmeno tecnicamente. È proprio in periodo di austerità che l'arte deve servire a qualcosa, e torna così ad inseguire una sua propria funzionalità – anche quando la totale perdita del reale la obbliga ad essere una funzionalità irrazionale. Per questo motivo il linguaggio – la scrittura – entra a far parte del visivo, come veicolo e vettore informativo di default, come tentativo di incontrare più persone possibili. Fiato alle trombe: questo è il gran ritorno nella nostra società di quella tecnologia (molto anni '90) conosciuta come OCR – quella che ci permette di scannerizzare un'immagine e leggerla come testo... J. mi ha detto che ogni opera è un dono che si fa al mondo. Mi son poi accorto strada facendo che – come ogni dono che si rispetti – è avvolto in una carta-regalo, e quelle persone che lo spacchettano per sapere cosa c'è dentro sono i nostri simili. Ho immaginato che un'opera d'arte potesse essere un ponte levatoio per favorire questo incontro con i propri simili – e solo di recente mi sono ricreduto: non è un ponte levatoio ma un trampolino, e se l'incontro avviene, allora avviene in totale assenza di architettura – avviene a mezz'aria.

Techno Casa – Allegato 4,82 Kb

Camminavo nel parco monumentale – di notte – non smetteva da tre giorni di nevicare. Notavo una strana alleanza tra le sculture bronzee e i sempreverdi. Tutto al buio e tutto ricoperto di neve. Non capivo chi imitava cosa. Se le sculture prendessero le sembianze della natura – oppure se gli alberi (flirtando con la mia immaginazione) non stessero prendendo in giro le sculture stesse, educandole alla gioia di vivere. Forse è tutto dovuto all'ambivalenza con cui la neve ricopre la città. Tutto è bianco – e quindi tendenzialmente tutto più calcolabile. Però le distanze, le presenze, i piani scompaiono – e non c'è più niente da calcolare – se non il tempo. Nell'iridescenza di una superficie che non rimane uguale a se stessa nemmeno per un istante – la facilità con cui si collegano i punti di riferimento è fomentata dalla totale scomparsa di ogni punto di riferimento. Uscendo dal parco, alla mia destra trovo il palazzo di vetro della CDU – l'unione dei cristiano-democratici tedeschi, cui massimo esponente è l'attuale Cancelliere Angela Merkel. Ed è proprio nei vetri di questo palazzo che vedo riflessa l'architettura antistante, il Museo del Bauhaus. E a questo punto s'insinua un dubbio nella mia mente: la vicinanza di queste due architetture – una di fronte all'altra – può essere del tutto casuale, oppure fanno parte di un unico piano? E forse questo piano è ben più ampio del piano regolatore cittadino? Una cosa mi è chiara: il palazzo di rappresentanza della forza di maggioranza parlamentare – e il corrispettivo palazzo di rappresentanza del movimento artistico che fece dell'utilitarismo il suo stendardo – si sono dati appuntamento qui, a questo semaforo, a questo incrocio. Che cosa dovranno dirsi – o meglio – cosa devono dire a me che sono arrivato ora? Se è vero che il telefono cellulare ha sostituito l'arredamento nell'intermediazione tra noi e lo spazio circostante, è altrettanto vero che la politica (non il web) è divenuta l'unica vera interfaccia tecnologica globale. Ne deduco che il palazzo della CDU e il Museo del Bauhaus – la strana coppia (join-venture) – sia coalizzata attorno alla condivisione del medesimo interesse: garantire il fatto che il suo popolo (target) continui a credere nell'interattività tecnologica – e di conseguenza nella rappresentanza parlamentare. In questi giorni le rivoluzioni, così come le democrazie, sembrano voler modificare la percezione con cui il mondo guarda a loro stesse in qualità di eventi – e non sembrano invece voler migliorare le condizioni di vita degli esseri umani che le vivono. Per questo motivo l'interattività tecnologica, vista da qui, è un falso mito. Si propone di circoscrivere numericamente le soluzioni – lasciando intendere che così facendo si possano eliminare alcuni problemi. E circoscrivere numericamente i problemi, in pratica, non è che la riproposizione del metodo più antico di cancellazione totale delle minoranze – quel metodo che disidrata la vita dai fiumi della paura e dai vortici dell'incalcolabile. Sul piano lavorativo – questo metodo si traduce nella parcellizzazione infinitesimale delle professioni e dei professionismi. In questo modo ogni categoria o campo del sapere può rimandare ad altre categorie o campi del sapere la ricerca di un risultato soddisfacente ogni volta che un dubbio o un'ipotesi rischia di mettere in discussione la sua logica interna. In pratica si rimanda costantemente – e così facendo – si finisce nei meandri di una costante e patologica smania da previsione. Chiedersi cosa succederà è il metodo più semplice, in pratica, per dimenticarsi cosa sta succedendo. Ma questo coinvolge chiunque e non passa mai di moda, ed è riscontrabile in ogni persona che – si dice – possiede delle priorità. Nuvole di senso si fingono geometrie solide – e poi si vendono a noi come scale di valori... ma cosa s'intende esattamente quando si parla di scala di valori? S'intende Il tempo con cui una persona (a seconda dell'agilità e delle contingenze) riesce a salir o scendere da questa scala più o meno velocemente. Si può costruire una scala di valori solo ammettendo che mancheranno sempre dei gradini – e che questo causa buchi e vuoti che non sono mai dove ce li ricordiamo – e questa scala, per giunta, è senza passamano. Nell'iridescenza di una superficie che non rimane uguale a se stessa nemmeno per un istante – la facilità con cui si collegano i punti di riferimento è fomentata dalla totale scomparsa di ogni punto di riferimento. Al momento siamo tutti impossibilitati – a differenza della neve – ad aver cura di ogni cosa.

Techno Casa – Allegato 5,53 Kb

Il giorno in cui son nato, mio padre aveva un po' timore del fatto che io potessi nascere con le orecchie a sventola come le sue – che da ragazzo i suoi amici lo chiamavano Dumbo. Quando mio nonno arrivò in ospedale – mio padre lo accolse sorridendo – era felice, certo felice anche per la dimensione contenuta dei miei padiglioni auricolari. Il padre di mio padre gli mise una mano sulla spalla (me lo immagino beffardo) e disse a suo figlio di non preoccuparsi: quelle piccole orecchie, le mie piccole orecchie, si sarebbero aperte come due roselline al sole. E ancora oggi, piuttosto che stare lì impalato a guardare gli alberi che cercano ostinatamente di stare in fila contro la tempesta, o i gabbiani che si avvicinano alla spiaggia senza nemmeno sbattere le ali, preferisco che siano le mie orecchie a dare forma al vento. Perché se le idee rimangono nell'aria, si dice, non è mai merito del vento – ma delle orecchie prima, e delle bocche poi. Quando si dorme un'orecchia è sempre appoggiata al cuscino, e quindi ci è impossibile sentire suoni stereo. Forse ci si incontra e accoppia proprio per scappare da questa trappola unidirezionale, per scegliere un compagno di sonno che offra un altro paio di orecchie, e ci riporti a sentire normalmente anche quando dormiamo (e si potrebbe arrivare a dire che la stessa trappola unidirezionale – monocanale – viene ribadita dalla sostituzione dello sguardo umano con quello della webcam). Forse il divincolarsi dei rami degli alberi non è dovuto al sole – e al loro tentativo di esporsi ai suoi raggi – e forse nemmeno al vento. I rami degli alberi crescono seguendo il movimento delle nuvole: quelli che puntano verso il basso sono nati probabilmente d'inverno, cercando di inseguire il manifestarsi del vero – terreno – all'andarsene della nebbia. Ogni ramo ha memoria della sua nuvola, e giorno dopo giorno la rintraccia e scruta sforzandosi di indicarla agli altri rami, a loro volta intenti con le loro nuvole. Non si può arrivare a parlare di un vero e proprio tentativo di fuga dal tronco, ma di certo senza la testardaggine dei rami noi rimarremmo qui, all'oscuro del costante peregrinare delle nuvole. Il vento che muove le nuvole e le foglie degli alberi produce un suono molto simile a quello delle onde del mare che portano i detriti sul bagnasciuga – ed entrambi i movimenti, da molti punti di vista, scandiscono il tempo. Però il vento è imprevedibile – ci conduce verso una ripetitività incalcolabile alla quale non ci si può abituare. E a proposito: noi siamo stati educati a ripetere dei gesti – oppure qualcuno ha tentato di trasmetterci delle idee che li sottendono, al fine di dare vita a gesti senza precedenti? Ognuno perdona qualcosa a chi lo precede e ognuno regala qualcosa a chi gli succede. Abbiamo perdonato loro di aver creduto alla favola della moltiplicazione dei pani e dei pesci – perché ci siamo accorti che è un raffinato stratagemma basato sul fatto che le briciole sono divisibili all'infinito. E abbiamo perdonato loro anche l'idea secondo la quale mettersi tutti d'accordo sarebbe stato poi semplice – perché ci è chiaro che ci si può mettere tutti d'accordo solo quando ci sono degli assenti. Adesso non ci resta che dare forma al vento, origliando quel chiacchiericcio quotidiano che ogni foglia intraprende con il suo ramo. Ognuno perdona qualcosa a chi lo precede e ognuno regala qualcosa a chi gli succede. E poi salvar qualcosa magari, nel passaggio che dalle braccia porta alla mente – da bracciante agricolo a lavoratore cognitivo indipendente. Dal tempo delle stagioni al tempo delle macchine e poi al tempo della mente: ascoltare il vento come formula provvisoria – invisibili barricate contro la colonizzazione dell'istante. Dal tempo delle stagioni al tempo delle macchine e poi al tempo della mente: l'agricoltura dopo il matrimonio con la meccanica si è risposata con la chimica – una ragazza apparentemente di meno pretese. L'agricoltura nei panni di quel marito – quel marito che per avere la botte piena e la moglie ubriaca, ha infilato la moglie nella botte, per poi accorgersi che così non ci avrebbe più fatto all'amore. L'amore come intima sfida al tempo che passa – e allo stesso tempo – solidificazione del suo labirinto, attraverso una reciproca esternazione di sensazioni sottocutanee.

Techno Casa – Allegato 6,69 Mb

Sto osservando una goccia di olio di oliva che, a partire dal mio polso, si fa strada nell'avambraccio fino ad arrivare al gomito – dove sogna di trasformarsi in stalattite, nonostante stia visibilmente perdendo volume e consistenza lungo il tragitto che disegna fra i pori della mia pelle. Seguendo la goccia nel suo rimpicciolirsi mi dico che io – quotidianamente – lavoro per l'Agenzia dei Rifiuti. Ogni volta che gestisco la raccolta differenziata della mia spazzatura, lavoro per l'Agenzia dei Rifiuti e lei non mi paga. Mi da particolarmente fastidio spendere tempo in questo, così come dover infilare le mani in un sacchetto di plastica che diffonde l'olezzo di diversi contenitori per alimenti. Mi è stato consigliato – proprio dall'Agenzia dei Rifiuti – di lavare questi contenitori, queste scatole dall'aria affranta che ai miei occhi sembrano umide bare in attesa del ritorno dei loro cadaveri. Dovrei quindi detergere la spazzatura differenziata prima di metterla nel sacchetto che conservo nel mobile sotto il lavandino – e visto che il packaging è stato fatto per i miei occhi – pare che non ci sia alcun dubbio: è proprio compito mio lavarlo. In pratica detergo, divido, imbusto e poi ridivido nell'apposito cassonetto perché responsabilizzarsi rispetto alla spazzatura che si produce è un passo necessario alla sopravvivenza del pianeta. La pensano così anche le più ricche multinazionali del settore alimentare, anticipando spesso nella realtà dei fatti l'applicazione di una futura teoria legislativa a riguardo. Una ditta che produce una famosa bevanda gassata – per esempio – in un paese del Sud America ha attivato un progetto pilota di recupero delle proprie bottiglie direttamente dai Waste Pickers – una classe particolarmente disagiata di lavoratori autonomi – la cui principale mansione è esattamente quella di cui, poco fa, mi lamentavo. Ognuno dei Waste Pickers ha una zona – spesso una strada – di riferimento. Si presentano al mattino davanti casa a recuperare la spazzatura di ogni famiglia – che forse magari chissà li ringrazia – ma di certo non li paga per questo (esattamente come l'Agenzia dei Rifiuti con me). Poi i Waste Pickers passano la giornata a smistare il contenuto dei sacchetti – anticipando il gesto con cui la sera stessa divideranno e incolonneranno una sopra all'altra – a seconda del taglio – le monete, i centesimi guadagnati per aver venduto plastica, metallo, vetro, carta alle ditte di riciclatori. F. mi racconta che è impossibile – per via delle attuali norme sull'igiene – immaginare che la ditta che produce la famosa bevanda gassata stia ricomprando le proprie bottiglie per poi lavarle e riutilizzarle. E allo stesso tempo ribadisce F. – è altrettanto impensabile che la ditta le ritiri dal mercato per trasformarle poi in materia grezza con la quale rifondere nuove bottiglie – perché ci sono altre ditte specializzate in questo settore che possono offrire il servizio a prezzi decisamente più contenuti. Allora dico a F. – si potrebbe immaginare che il vero motivo sia un tentativo di digitalizzare la realtà attraverso la spazzatura. La ditta che produce la famosa bevanda gassata infatti – raccogliendo le proprie bottiglie dai Waste Pickers – ottiene informazioni spazio-temporali sul consumo del proprio prodotto, perché è in grado di risalire (con un'approssimazione molto vicina alla realtà) a dove la bevanda è stata consumata e in quanto tempo – quando è stata definitivamente bevuta l'ultima goccia di famosa bevanda ormai non più gassata? Ottenuti questi dati e messi in relazione con i dati di produzione e distribuzione la ditta sarà in grado di prevedere il desiderio di bevanda gassata – ottenendo un potere magico lucrativo per via di una vorace lungimiranza, a sua volta sostenuta da un calcolo matematicamente intransigente presentato in forma di sentimento ecologista. E ogni volta che navigo su internet permetto a chiunque di prevedere un mio desiderio. Ogni gesto del mio dito – conosciuto come click – produce per qualcun altro un'informazione e quindi un guadagno in divenire: ecco come le regole del web sono trasferite alla realtà – a tutti gli effetti fenomenica – della spazzatura. Ai consumatori (user) questo processo concede di dare senso al proprio tempo libero trasformandolo in lavoro gratuito, e dividere – definitivamente e per sempre – l'idea di produttività da quella di occupazione. Quindi non è più vero che si paga tutto, specialmente nel web ci sono sempre più servizi gratuiti, ma lo sono perché abbiamo accettato inconsciamente l'idea di un volontariato obbligatorio ed espanso. Tra l'altro, dare senso al proprio tempo libero trasformandolo in lavoro gratuito è un'attività che fino a poco fa era concessa esclusivamente alle classi nobili – ecco perché oggi ci proviamo tutti – click – e ci riusciamo tutti – doppio click. Questo è il pulpito da cui arriva la predica dell'intera classe media sulla propria sussistenza. Potremmo allora sostituire la domanda: da che pulpito viene la predica? Con la domanda: da che predica viene il pulpito? Mi fermo per un istante e mi pento addirittura di essermi lamentato per l'assenza di tempo a mia disposizione, ma proprio intanto che mi sto riappacificando mentalmente con l'Agenzia dei Rifiuti mi sfugge da ogni controllo un gesto incondizionato del collo – e mi ritrovo a leccare il mio avambraccio rimpossessandomi della goccia d'olio di oliva smarrita.

– Ogni considerevole cambiamento nelle musiche di moda
è indice di un cambiamento nelle più importanti disposi-
zioni dello Stato.
– Come accade questa strana relazione? [...]
– Per "semplice radicamento". Si canticchia, si ascolta, si
ripete. Il nuovo ritmo si diffonde nella vita quotidiana dove
si fortifica.

Alain Badiou, La Repubblica di Platone

Qui si possono acquistare anche canzoni, che il negoziante
canta e il cliente deve tenere a mente; ma di solito è facile
tenerle a mente, trattandosi di canzoni vecchissime, dive-
nute noiose a forza di cantarle. Sono soprattutto i giova-
notti in amore che le comprano [...] Le canzoni sono alla
portata di tutti, e dopo averne acquistata una di solito il
giovane esce cantandola a voce spiegata. Il negoziante ac-
corre sulla porta per correggere qualche stonatura; ma il
giovane non lo ascolta e rifà la canzone a suo modo, mentre
va in giro cantandola per la città. Tutti sanno a cosa prelude
quel canto.

Gianni Celati, Fata Morgana

Techno Casa – Allegato 7,02 Mb

Più ascolto l'ultimo disco dei Daft Punk e più mi rendo conto che rappresenta una nuova idea di presente: come se fosse un documentario sonoro su ciò che è accaduto – ma realizzato con le orecchie del divenire. Codifica l'evento musicale in un precedente – lasciando assaporare così all'ascoltatore l'idea di esserne lui stesso la durata – il durante. Come se non si vendessero più i dischi, non si vendesse musica – ma si vendesse il sogno di diventare musicisti. Come se la rivoluzione digitale avesse ricoperto il pianeta con un'eterea superficie di equità – permettendo a chiunque di creare musica e farla sentire in giro attraverso il web. Ad un concerto per esempio, partecipano solo musicisti – e se si volesse dividerli in due gruppi si potrebbe farlo in musicisti attivi – sul palco – e musicisti passivi – sotto il palco. L'album dei Daft Punk è un disco educational – una miccia – ogni miccia è una catena – una miccia collegata a esplosivi sonori che al momento però sono solo in fase di studio. I laboratori in cui questi esplosivi sonori sono in fase di studio si chiamano precisamente stanze – e all'interno ci sono nuove generazioni di musicisti che in questo momento stanno muovendo la testa a ritmo della loro ultima creazione. Scuotono di vibrazioni l'intera casa – come se per viaggiare bastasse disintegrarla invece che uscirne! Questa però – va detto – è un'allucinazione creata dal fantasma che si annida in ogni strumento musicale, in ogni interfaccia tecnologica utilizzata per far musica. Questi strumenti infatti – da un lato arredano perfettamente la stanza (trovando in ogni luogo eletto il luogo ideale) – dall'altro lato sono stati creati per facilitare esigenze di trasporto, spesso esasperate fino al tascabile. Non a caso, che io sia a casa o fuori casa, il disco dei Daft Punk lo ascolto solo sullo smartphone – così come l'ultimo album di Jay-Z, uno dei mie rapper preferiti. Qui però il discorso è diverso, perché Jay-Z ha realizzato il suo ultimo disco attraverso una app prodotta esclusivamente per l'azienda che ha costruito e commercializzato il mio smartphone. La app mi ha permesso di downloadare il disco gratuitamente ben tre giorni prima della data di lancio ufficiale prevista dalla casa discografica e Jay-Z vede in questo metodo una genuina possibilità per riformulare le regole selvagge del web. È risaputo che internet è il territorio dei leaks – e che spesso gli album per cui c'è una grande attesa compaiono illegalmente in download gratuito ancora prima di essere realizzati. Si potrebbe dire che Jay-Z non ha fatto altro che vendere il leak dell'album a una multinazionale della telefonia – che a sua volta ha garantito al rapper l'acquisto anticipato di un milione di copie da regalare ai suoi clienti – me compreso. Così facendo Jay-Z ha assicurato al suo nuovo album lo status di disco di platino ancora prima che fosse uscito – creando un precedente nella storia della discografia. Il rapper – in poche parole – ha brandizzato un leak. E la sponsorizzazione di un leak – evoluzione in chiave autopoietica della banale vendita concordata dello scoop – deve aver fatto ragionare un caro amico di Jay-Z – nonché presidente degli Stati Uniti d'America. Se Barack Oh Blah Blah avesse seguito l'esempio del suo amico – brandizzando i numerosi leaks a cui ha fatto fronte il suo governo – avrebbe probabilmente potuto ricavare un gran beneficio economico, mi dico. Nel clima da sondaggio statistico permanente, l'idea è di rendere tutto mimetico e trasparente – vaporizzato: passano nuvole dello stesso colore del cielo – e come fai a vederle? Come se non si comprassero più i voti – ma si vendesse il sogno di diventare parlamentare. L'atteggiamento d'avanguardia nelle democrazie occidentali – la trasmutazione di una nuova tecnologia nella forma vivissima del partito politico – non è altro che l'affermazione del fatto che ogni tipo di astrazione può essere vissuta come la rappresentanza parlamentare – l'astrazione originaria. Scopro così che Jay-Z terrà un concerto in città e decido allora di inseguire la melodia – così come si fa quando si sente suonare un telefono che non è il proprio ma si vorrebbe comunque rispondere. Mi ritrovo in un lato della città da poco edificato e velocemente adibito a piazza, al fine di indirizzare lo sguardo di noi bipedi verso la facciata vitrea dell'arena che ospita i grandi eventi. Questo fabbricato sembra appena arrivato – e la polvere che ha alzato durante l'atterraggio si è trasformata immediatamente in cemento – immobilizzata in una parcellizzazione verticale degli spazi – bloccata nella forma della svendita. Come se non si affittassero più appartamenti, ma si vendesse il sogno di diventarne proprietari. Come se l'alleanza fra il settore immobiliare e la finanza – a fronte di un welfare al supplizio – avesse fluidificato il meccanismo della rivalsa sociale attraverso l'indebitamento privato, visto come ultimo metodo di accesso ad un bene comune. E quale sarà l'indirizzo di questi nuovi appartamenti in vendita? Quando – alla ricerca di una soluzione in forma di cartello toponomastico – la trovo – non voglio credere ai miei occhi: non solo il nome dell'arena – ma anche il nome della stessa piazza in cui l'architettura è sorta è esattamente il nome della mia compagnia telefonica, quella a cui pago la bolletta del telefono! Allora – frastornato – entro nell'arena e mi accorgo che tutto è organizzato attorno alla facciata trasparente, il cui vetro – ribadito con lo stratagemma della ripetizione a griglia – vorrebbe rimandare alla possibilità che il mondo qui dentro sia una buona rappresentazione del mondo là fuori. Sono circondato da nuovi materiali costruttivi miserabili – resi organici da un turbinio di led come a manifestare un perfetto connubio tra risparmio energetico e spreco semiotico – come se la Casa Bianca, per esempio, si chiamasse così perché è completamente realizzata in cartongesso. Poi fortunatamente tutto sparisce: si spengono le luci e si accendono le migliaia tascabili – Jay-Z entra in scena e io mi lascio abbracciare dal boato generale – ogni concerto è la meta narrazione che gli smartphones che vi partecipano offrono di sé.

Techno Casa – Allegato 8,88 Mb

Controllo le news sul mio smartphone ogni tre minuti, leggo solo i titoli e non approfondisco – mi assicuro che il mondo, là fuori, non cambi – o mi accerto che se eventualmente là fuori dovesse succedere qualcosa, allora che almeno un po' mi riguardi. Raramente mi concedo un giornale cartaceo, ma quando capita che io lo abbia fra le mani lo tratto come un bene di lusso e ne ispeziono i minimi particolari. Fra le varie pubblicità che si contendono l'angolo della pagina del quotidiano che ora sto sfogliando – una in particolare ha attirato la mia attenzione. Si tratta di una ditta che è specializzata nella trasformazione in doccia di qualunque vasca da bagno preesistente. Ci penso un attimo e mi dico che non avevo mai preso in considerazione questa possibilità – trasformare la vasca da bagno in una doccia. In effetti – al di là di chi ha problemi motori, oppure di chi possiede la Jacuzzi – chi è che si fa più il bagno? Penso a K. – K. è tra le poche persone che conosco che ancora possiedono una vasca da bagno. Un giorno mi ha rivelato che d'inverno – a fronte di una giornata di successo lavorativo, si concede un premio speciale facendosi un lungo bagno nell'acqua bollente dopo aver spento il suo smartphone. Ricordo che quando K. mi ha dato in mano il suo nuovo smartphone, si è assicurata – arrossendo lievemente – che io avessi le mani pulite. Poi mi ha detto di non badare al disordine – di non far caso alle stupide app che aveva sparse qua e là: le aveva downloadate per suo figlio che ogni tanto ci gioca. Ricordo che quando K. mi ha invitato ad andare a cena con la scusa di farmi vedere la sua nuova casa – non appena varcata la soglia dell'appartamento mi ha chiesto – arrossendo lievemente – di togliermi le scarpe. Poi mi ha detto di non badare al disordine – fingendo a tratti di rincorrerne l'artefice che – a giudizio unanime degli adulti presenti – era suo figlio – nascosto ora dietro la lavatrice in cucina. K. mi dice che non ha potuto scegliere, quando si è trasferita in quell'appartamento c'erano già entrambe – la vasca da bagno e la doccia – e quindi la vasca da bagno se l'è tenuta, e invece che non usarla per niente almeno la usa ogni tanto. La vasca occupa più di due metri quadrati – rendendo la stanza da bagno meno agibile e più piccola – ecco perché la lavatrice è in cucina. Ora che riguardo con attenzione l'inserzione pubblicitaria della ditta che trasforma le vasche da bagno in docce – noto che nel logo c'è un uomo che appoggia una sorta di sportello lucido sulla vasca da bagno. È un tecnico ben preparato quest'uomo – e lo si capisce dal fatto che ha una tuta da lavoro rossa con bretelle incrociate sulla schiena – immagine che rimanda subito alla coerenza del lavoro fisico e manuale. Faccio una ricerca su internet attraverso il mio smartphone e – in attesa che la pagina web compaia – noto che l'icona circolare che gira su se stessa al centro dello schermo assomiglia allo sportello di una lavatrice in funzione. La pagina web della ditta finalmente si apre, e scopro che il tempo necessario all'uomo con la tuta rossa per trasformare una vasca da bagno in doccia sono esattamente 8 ore. Immagino che a quell'uomo dopo le 8 ore di lavoro – ne rimangano altre 8 per lo svago, e ancora 8 per dormire... ma sento già di sbagliarmi nel preciso momento in cui lo penso. Questa scansione delle 24 ore in tre blocchi da 8 ore ciascuno – appartiene ad un periodo storico in cui negli appartamenti non esistevano le docce, ma solo le vasche da bagno – mi dico. È successo in pratica che la vasca da bagno si è alzata in piedi – divenendo doccia – proprio quando il numero 8, stanco di sè e del suo stesso ripetersi, si è accasciato su se stesso – divenendo, più o meno così ∞ – il simbolo dell'infinito. Il numero 8 infatti non ha mai potuto riposarsi – e solo ora che la vasca da bagno si è alzata in piedi, lui ha lo spazio per stendersi – così ∞. E non mi stupirei domani di scoprire che altri amici – per evitare di installare la lavatrice in cucina e per lasciare riposare all'∞ il numero 8 – decidessero di non possedere né la vasca da bagno né la doccia – perché si possono lavare in palestra, in piscina, al lavoro. All'idea di arredo (dell'appartamento con i mobili) si potrebbe sostituire l'idea di customizzazione (dello smartphone con le app) – come se svuotare la propria casa da oggetti divenuti inutili invece che accumularne sia la formula per non invecchiare mai.

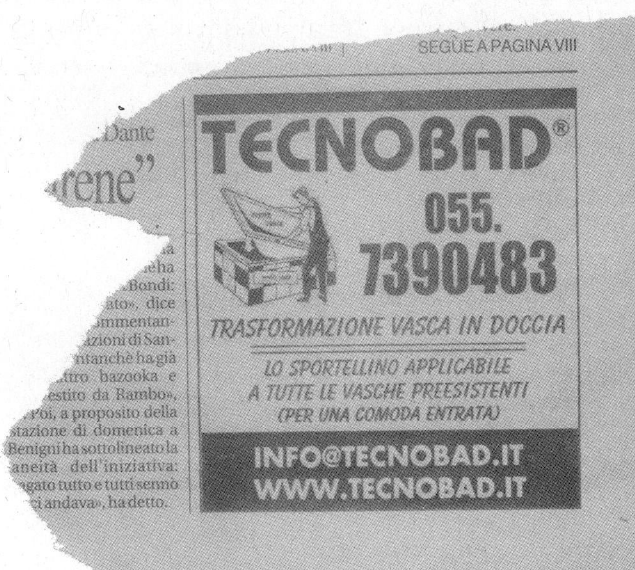

Techno Casa – Allegato 9,24 Mb

Ieri ho comprato delle sigarette di una marca che non avevo mai provato prima, perché quella che io fumo di solito non era disponibile. Aprendo il pacchetto, con meraviglia, ci ho trovato dentro un messaggio. Su un cartoncino a sfondo blu, che richiama immediatamente la bandiera dell'Europa, campeggiava un'affermazione e poi una domanda: Fumatori discriminati! Cos'altro? Poi girandolo mi accorgo che è una vera e propria lamentela nei confronti delle regolamentazioni che l'Unione Europea sta formulando sulla somministrazione di tabacco, lamentela che chiosa in una spiegazione perentoria che mi ha fatto sorridere e presagire la nascita di un sindacato dei fumatori sovvenzionato dalle ditte produttrici di sigarette. La frase sul cartoncino recita: noi pensiamo che l'Unione Europea debba preoccuparsi di cose più importanti! Questa è un'affermazione talmente generica che non può che trovare tutti d'accordo, e identificandoli come gruppo di consumatori – non fa che ricordare agli Europei a che cosa serve l'Europa. Un'idea d'Europa talmente generica che non può che trovare tutti d'accordo. Mi chiedo cosa davvero accomuna queste Nazioni che si sono unite e mi domando se, quando si sta insieme, si sta insieme per raggiungere il meglio o si sta insieme per dividersi il peggio. Per esempio, se io dico: difficilmente semplice! – E poi dico: semplicemente difficile! – Perché vince sempre il male? Ora ripenso a R. – che mi ha raccontato che fuma moltissime sigarette – godendosele molto – ma solo in sogno. Forse R. ha trovato la soluzione ad ogni male? Se dovessi sforzarmi di trovare ciò che accomuna queste Nazioni Europee non potrei che pensare all'architettura dei quartieri periferici – e al suo essere riflesso volumetrico di un processo d'astrazione che ci ha accompagnato fino a qui per poi farci scendere anche se non è il capolinea. Processo d'astrazione che ha portato ad investire non più su beni tangibili (la casa) – ma su beni immateriali (stock finanziari) – processo che si è poi piegato su se stesso proprio perché il bene immobile – così evidentemente immobile nei quartieri periferici – è rimasto nel tempo il terreno fertile sul quale coltivare speranze. L'amore infatti, dopo essersi condensato nell'atto della creazione di una nuova famiglia, si cristallizza nell'architettura rappresentata dalla nuova casa. Le famiglie hanno iniziato a lavorare in fabbrica

– dalle campagne si sono spostate in città – portatrici di vita in zone liminari, ora urbanizzate con solerzia – ritagliate di sghembo con la forbice del piano urbanistico – e poi mestamente incollate attorno ad arterie stradali (simbolo di civiltà). Si chiamano quartieri dormitorio perché – chi ci vive – passa la vita a sognare. Nei quartieri dormitorio, maggiore è la vicinanza con uno snodo di traffico privilegiato e maggiore è il costo dell'abitazione, al di là delle sue peculiarità specifiche. La deformazione antropologica di una specie inizia con la constatazione del fatto che un balcone che si affaccia sulla fermata della metropolitana o dell'autobus è preferibile ad un balcone che si affaccia sull'aperta campagna – anche perché, si dice, in quei campi non coltivati presto sorgeranno nuovi palazzi. Quindi il balcone che si affaccia sulla fermata della metropolitana non solo offre un paesaggio sicuro e stabile, ma certifica – come un matrimonio o un funerale – il compimento di un destino. Ma al di là del trasporto pubblico – che non basta a rispondere alle nuove esigenze e non glorifica certo il compimento di un destino – l'asfalto è arrivato lì come piedistallo su cui esibire autovetture: il loro luccichio cromato moltiplica perfettamente i riflessi accecanti del sogno che si aggira zitto zitto fra i parcheggi: aree mute con lampioni soli che si guardano attorno come se qualcosa potesse cambiare, lampioni che fanno la corte agli alberi senza accorgersi che non potrà mai funzionare. Le automobili cambiano la scala dimensionale: i loro interni in pelle allungano fuori dalle stanze – verso la società – i divani in pelle: come se ci si potessero sedere più persone sullo stesso divano ma senza stringersi. E i parcheggi quindi si ripetono, uno dopo l'altro, con grande fame di vetture – e spesso circondano la base dei palazzi e attestano che l'edilizia sociale è ben piantata in terra. E intanto – là nelle fabbriche – le macchine funzionano così bene che funzionano troppo (sovrapproduzione). Le macchine per i lavoratori – così come per le mogli le badanti (extracomunitarie) – arrivano come aiutanti ma poi diventano sostitute. E saranno le macchine stesse ad interpretare una nuova tipologia di processo clorofilliano – come i lampioni che flirtano con gli alberi nei parcheggi... Davvero pensavi che gli alberi arrossissero solo d'autunno? Così come la vegetazione fu necessaria all'uomo (nutrendosi di anidride carbonica – che l'essere umano espelle – ma espellendo ossigeno – di cui l'essere umano necessita per vivere) allo stesso modo le macchine sono necessarie all'uomo, perché si nutrono di tempo qualitativo – che l'essere umano espelle – ed espellono tempo numerico – che l'essere umano necessita per vivere meglio, fare più cose, e continuare disperatamente a prendersela con il tempo che passa come se si fossero perse indecifrabili fortune. E potrei anche continuare – ma fumo l'ultima sigaretta e poi devo andare.

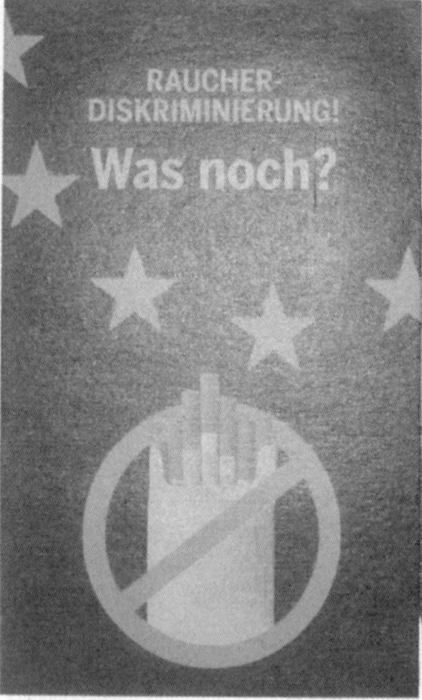

RAUCHER-
DISKRIMINIERUNG!

Was noch?

DIE EU WILL:

GROSSE SCHOCKFOTOS AUF
DEN PACKUNGEN ZEIGEN

MENTHOLZIGARETTEN
UND SLIMS VERBIETEN

WIR DENKEN:
Die EU hat sich um Wichtigeres
zu kümmern!

Verbot stoppen
und handeln unter:
www.was-noch.eu

Techno Casa – Allegato 10,01 Mb

Osservo l'evolvere del temporale estivo oltre la finestra. Metto a fuoco un palazzo ed escludo dal mio sguardo tutto quello che lì attorno – ogni giorno – soffre e gode a rotazione della sua ombra. Benché alle spalle dell'edificio le nuvole s'inseguano, si mischino in nuove configurazioni antropomorfe e poi si lascino repentinamente per sempre, io ho la netta sensazione che siano ferme – e che sia il palazzo a muoversi. Così come sul treno fermo in stazione percepisco un finto movimento dovuto dal fatto che – oltre il finestrino – una carrozza sul binario attiguo è già partita, allo stesso modo qui il palazzo è il protagonista in perenne movimento sul palco, mentre il cielo è immobile, il più antico dei fondali teatrali. Non appena il temporale si zittisce – per riprendermi qualche attimo di vita in questa morte da scrivania – decido di andare a correre nel parco. Mi bagno di una pioggia di cui mi sto già dimenticando e trovo il parco lugubre, una

pozza d'acqua in totale assenza degli schiamaz-
zi dei bambini, avvolto nell'ombra dei cantieri
di altri nuovi palazzi. D'un tratto mi è chiaro ciò
che spinge gli sperduti passeggiatori solitari, anziani apparentemente sfaccendati, ad osservare
con tanto interesse quei cantieri: in quegli istanti,
dettati dal ritmo della meccanica edile, l'architettura è viva – dove la messa in cantiere è messa in
scena – movimento. Le gru che si muovono sono
vettori metallici che localizzano geograficamente
la novità, e il loro albero centrale (asse delle x)
ne fissa le radici mentre il braccio che si distacca
dal corpo (asse delle y) ne annuncia prematura-
mente i confini. Correndo mi accorgo che davanti
a me in lontananza, alcuni raggi di sole si sono
fatti strada al tramonto, ed illuminano esclusivamente una panchina che sembra grande come un
regno e abitata temporaneamente da una regina
che – avvolta in un bozzolo invisibile ma iride-
scente – legge un importantissimo libro. Sbircian-
dola da lontano – nella prospettiva concessa dalla
mia corsa – non solo mi è sembrato di conoscerla,
ma ho avuto anche la sensazione – del tutto fal-
sa – che lei stesse leggendo il libro della mia vita.
Quando il mio corpo, correndo, è entrato in quel
fascio di luce ho girato le spalle alla regina – che
nel frattempo avrebbe potuto anche essersi dis-
solta – e il mio viso si è girato di scatto al cospetto
del sole – i miei occhi hanno incontrato la fonte
dei raggi e tentato disperatamente di mettere a

fuoco la forma sferica tremante. Potrei dire che ciò che ho provato, nel sentire le mucose del mio naso asciugarsi in un istante e distillare gocce di piacere giù nella gola – è stata una sensazione del tutto simile ad un orgasmo – amplificata dal mio essere totalmente sudato e sotto sforzo per la corsa. Da quel momento in poi, il tragitto della corsa è stato dettato dalla ricerca di quella sensazione – che ho avuto modo di riprovare, non diluita ma intensificata dall'assenza di sorpresa ribadita nella ripetizione. Il passare del tempo, così come il viaggiare nello spazio – mi son detto – obbligano a mettersi a proprio agio. A volte, la prima cosa che si fa è ritrovare sensazioni che si conoscono già, ma in tempi nuovi – o ricollocare cose appurate in luoghi mai attraversati prima. Si rivedono i tratti somatici del migliore amico in un passante, o si respira l'arietta di primavera anche se è la fine dell'estate – si cerca in qualche modo di ambientarsi. E ci si appiglia a tutto, ma proprio a tutto: più la realtà diviene invivibile e più ci s'inventa qualcosa che non esiste, o piuttosto, ci si sforza di intravedere qualcosa che non è ancora successo ma che allo stesso tempo è un misto di cose date per scontate. Questa, si potrebbe dire, è la formula con cui – all'apice di un'esigenza – avviene qualcosa di nuovo. Qualcosa che non è ancora successo ma che allo stesso tempo è un misto di cose date per scontate. E addirittura questo è il vettore con cui noi esseri umani andiamo in direzione di una vita migliore. E proprio per questi motivi l'amore non può che essere un lento scivolare all'indietro – o una corsa in costante controtempo, che ci riporta al punto dal quale siamo partiti. Da dove siamo partiti? Siamo partiti addormentandoci con i piedi avviluppati ma dandoci le spalle. La sera dopo invece siamo caduti nel sonno sfiorandoci la bocca per non perder nemmeno un istante. La giornata più lunga dell'anno senza chiamarla solstizio. Al mattino poi, l'unica cosa che era lì a dimostrarci che il tempo non si era del tutto fermato, era la barba leggermente cresciuta e il non saper rispondere a quel nuovo solletico nell'interno coscia. Anni dopo – camminando per strada di notte – abbiamo riparlato di quel momento osservandolo in un oggetto ben preciso che emergeva da un palazzo storico. Un'antica meridiana era stata installata sulle spalle dell'edificio del Museo. Un apposito lampione – piazzato lì davanti sul palazzo antistante – la illuminava con un cerchio. Così la meridiana segnava sempre e solo un unico orario, per sempre – tutta la notte, perché illuminata da un oggetto fermo – il lampione – invece che dall'instancabile sole. E questo lampione che ne metteva in luce l'aspetto in realtà sottolineava il suo essere posticcia – cortocircuitandone la funzione. Poi ancora il temporale, e ci siamo bagnati di una pioggia di cui ci stavamo già dimenticando.

I wrote the texts of this book between 2011 and 2013 as an integral part of a body of work composed as a series of video-essays that have been presented in different site-specific installations and events. Every video – except for the introductory one – is called "Attachment" and has a numeric suffix that pretends to indicate a quantity of bits even if its own function is a mere indexical one. The Attachment with the suffix in "Kb" has been produced by Xing for the festival Gianni Peng / Live Arts Week II and presented through out a performative environment. The Attachment with the suffix in "Mb" has been subsequently produced by Gallerie d'Arte Moderna e Contemporanea, Ferrara, for the occasion of Art Fall '13, curated by Maria Luisa Pacelli.

In knowing that to translate someone else's work is a particular form of psychoanalysis, I particularly want to thanks Filipa Ramos and David Smith – as much as the photographers listed below – for staying on my side, looking at the world with my eyes, for their care and consistence.

The images appearing along the text are specifically conceived previously unpublished evidences I have been collecting during the voyage. While the photographic images dividing the english translation from the original italian text are documenting three different appearances of the Techno Casa project in the above mentioned occasion curated by Xing (2013) as much as at the Marsèlleria space in Milano (2013) and at PAC - Contemporary Art Pavillion of Milano (2014) on the occasion of Glitch curated by Davide Giannella. From page 47 to page 55 and from page 57 to 58 photo © Dario Lasagni. Page 56 photo © Gaetano Cammarota. From page 59 to page 67 and from page 69 to page 73, and pages 76 and 77 photo © Carola Merello. Pages 74 and 75 photo © Francesca Verga. From page 74 to page 79 photo © Marica Martella.

Thanks to all the fellows travellers for the contributions, discussions and support, including my students and Marianna Liosi, Andrea Lissoni, Silvia Fanti, Daniele Caspar Gasparinetti, Maria Luisa Pacelli, Mirko Rizzi, Alberto Salvadori, Filipa Ramos, Marco Ghigi, Jimmie Durham and Maria Thereza Alves, Margareth Kammerer, Jurij Magoga, Luigi Nerone, Franco Berardi Bifo, Federico Demaria, Gian Marco Vidor, Gianni Celati, Brandon LaBelle, Liam Gillick, Gyonata Bonvicini, Pier Luigi Guerrini, Dario Lasagni, Martina Angelotti, Dj Soul Solgia, Gabriele Tosi, Sara Dolfi Agostini, Vanni Codeluppi, Fabio Santacroce, Elena Bordignon, Maddalena and Pietro Torrigiani, Paolo Sante Cisi, Claudio Musso, David Smith, Mario Covello.

Techno Casa
Riccardo Benassi

ISBN: 978-0-9889375-2-9
© the author

An introduction to and from *Attachment 1,12 Kb* to *Attachment 5,53 Kb*
translated by Filipa Ramos, from *Attachment 6,96 Mb* to *Attachment 10,01
Mb* translated by David Smith.

Errant Bodies Press: DOORMATS[5]
Los Angeles / Berlin
2015
www.errantbodies.org

Series editors: Riccardo Benassi and Brandon LaBelle
Printed: Druckhaus Köthen
Design: Riccardo Benassi

Focusing on contemporary issues, events, and discourses, DOORMATS
is a series of publications aimed at contributing to the now, talking about
issues that are present and that demand presence.

DOORMATS[1] - Franco Berardi Bifo
Skizo-Mails

DOORMATS[2] - Brandon LaBelle
Diary of an Imaginary Egyptian

DOORMATS[3] - Valentina Montero
*By Reason or By Force: The Chilean neoliberal model and its implications for
education and culture*

DOORMATS[4] - Fred Dewey
The School of Public Life

DOORMATS[5] - Riccardo Benassi
Techno Casa

DOORMATS[6] - Lucia Farinati / Claudia Firth
The Force of Listening